to Dad
from Robert
christmas 2010

Abide with Me

A PHOTOGRAPHIC JOURNEY THROUGH GREAT BRITISH HYMNS

Text by John H. Parker

PHOTOGRAPHY BY PAUL SEAWRIGHT

New Leaf Press

bide with Me:

PHOTOGRAPHIC JOURNEY THROUGH GREAT BRITISH HYMNS

t Printing: April 2009
ond Printing: September 2009

ver and book layout design by Todd Knowlton

less otherwise noted, Scripture taken from the New King James Version of the Bible.

ted by Mary Hollingsworth, Creative Enterprises. www.CreativeEnterprisesLtd.com

N-13: 978-0-89221-690-1
N-10: 0-89221-690-5
rary of Congress Catalog Number: 2009920404

ted in China

ase visit our website for other great titles: www.newleafpress.net

information regarding author interviews, please contact the publicity department at (870) 438-5288.

ACKNOWLEDGMENTS

The authors thank the following people and institutions for their valuable assistance:

Dr. Jerry Rushford of Pepperdine University, leading authority on British hymnwriters and hymn sites, for generously providing us with his research itinerary and information;

Mary Hollingsworth, text editor, for experienced and professional editing, insightful advice on writing, and encouragement;

President Tim Dudley, editor-in-chief Laura Welch, assistant editor Craig Froman, and the staff of New Leaf Publishing Group for accepting, shaping, and producing this book;

Dr. F. LaGard Smith, friend and widely-known author and speaker, for support and guidance;

The vicars, ministers, and other personnel of churches and homes associated with writers of British hymns for graciously welcoming and assisting us;

Lipscomb University, for a financial grant and other support on this project, and **Marie Byers,** reference librarian at Beaman Library of Lipscomb University and curator of its Bailey Hymnology collection, for her valuable assistance;

And especially our wives, **Jill Parker and Sarah Seawright,** for their patience and good cheer over these three years.

AUDIO ACKNOWLEDGMENTS

As you read John Parker and Paul Seawright's book, *Abide With Me*, and listen to the enclosed CD, you will notice that the tones and sounds of the recordings vary in nature. Efforts were made to emulate, as close as possible, how you would have heard the songs sung had you been there when they were first written and performed in the local church building, cathedral, or auditorium.

It is our hope that your enjoyment and imagination will be enhanced by the CD rendition while reading *Abide With Me* and pouring through these magnificent photos, taken and so graphically displayed by international photographer, Paul Seawright.

Our thanks and appreciation to Harding University for contributing the beautiful recordings of its Harding University Concert Choir on track numbers 4, 5, 6, 7, 10, 11, 12, 13, 16, 19, and 21.

Also thanks and appreciation to Bill Shockley from dallaschristiansound.com for track numbers 14, 15, 17, 18, 20, 22, and 23.

The same appreciation to studyjesus.com for its contribution of "Abide With Me," the title song as sung by The Jordanaires and Shannon Singers on track number 3.

To Matthew Hearn, Professor of English, Lipscomb University, for his soulful and soul-filled interpretation of "Caedmon's Hymn," track number 8.

And, lastly, it is my pleasure to be a part of this effort by including track numbers 1, 2, 9, and 24 from my "I'd Rather Have Jesus" album.

New Leaf Publishing Group deserves and is awarded sincerest acclamation possible for making this effort breathe.

God bless you as you look, listen, and read *Abide With Me*.

Sincerely,

Ray Walker of The Jordanaires

Paul Seawright is Chair of Photography at the University of Ulster in Belfast. His photographs have been exhibited worldwide and are held in many museum collections, including the San Franciso Museum of Modern Art and the Art Institute of Chicago. In 1997 he was awarded the Irish Museum of Modern Art/Glen Dimplex Prize for outstanding contribution to Irish Art. He has published photographic books on Ireland, Afghanistan, and Africa. He lives on the County Down coast in Northern Ireland with his wife Sarah and their three children.

John Parker is Professor of English at Lipscomb University in Nashville, Tennessee, where he teaches courses in Shakespeare and American literature. He also writes religious literature and provides services as an interim minister for churches of Christ. John and his wife Jill have traveled extensively in Europe and England as faculty in Study Abroad programs. They live in Nashville and also enjoy their farm in middle Tennessee with their daughter Sharon, their son Robert, and his wife Bria.

For
JILL AND SARAH

CONTENTS

The focus of *Abide with Me* is place—the places in England and Wales where the great British hymns were written and where the stories of the men and women who wrote them unfolded: Olney ("Amazing Grace"), Brighton ("Just As I Am"), Stoke Newington ("When I Survey the Wondrous Cross"), Broadhembury ("Rock of Ages"), and many others. This book shows and tells about those places and what you would see if you visited them.

On the north coast of England, silhouetted against the gray sky and the dark sea, stand the ruins of Whitby Abbey. There in the sixth century a common sheep herder named Caedmon wrote the earliest surviving hymn written in English. In the centuries following—Middle Ages, Renaissance, Eighteenth Century, Nineteenth Century—men and women devoted to Christ and blessed with the gift of poetry composed the words of the English hymns sung in Britain, in America, and across the globe, generation after generation—sung in times of happiness, grief, joy, fear, and wonder. Here are the places those writers lived and their life stories.

Join us now for a stroll through the quaint Cotswolds, the beautiful Lake District, bustling London, and the glorious poppy-bedecked English countryside as you meet the great minds whose works have inspired, uplifted, and carried us through the tragedies and triumphs of our lives. It's a journey of the heart and soul—a meandering through your own spirituality.

Speaking to one another in psalms
and hymns and spiritual songs.
Ephesians 5:19

9

Olney, on the Ouse River in Northampton, England, not far from Cambridge, was a small farming and crafts village in the late eighteenth century. As we drive into the market square this Sunday afternoon, we find a bustling and cheerful town with two popular claims. One is the annual pancake race on Shrove Tuesday when housewives run 415 yards from the marketplace to the Church of St. Peter and St. Paul, each carrying a pan holding a pancake, which she flips on crossing the finish line. The other is the curate and preacher for that church from 1764–1780, John Newton (1725–1807), and the vicarage, where he wrote perhaps the most popular hymn of all time, "Amazing Grace."

The church was expanded during those years to accommodate the crowds who came to hear John, and its square tower still rises over the Ouse River. The sanctuary is large and impressive, and a stained-glass window commemorates the preacher and his hymn. Still, time has encroached a bit. His pulpit is now somewhat pushed back into a corner, though JOHN NEWTON'S PULPIT is proudly displayed along one edge. John's rather smallish portrait hangs on the stone buttress of one wall, sharing space between a fire extinguisher and a bulletin board where his name promotes a ministry in Sierra Leone. But after 230 years, it's still John Newton whose story and hymn live on here.

John was born to a master mariner, who was often away at sea, and a mother who taught him Bible lessons and the hymns of Isaac Watts (see pages 38-41). But she died when he was only six years old. At age eleven, after a few years of living with relatives or attending boarding school, he began sailing with his father.

In time John fell in love with Mary Catlett, daughter of friends of his mother, but in 1744 he was forced to serve on a naval ship. He records that while watching England's coast fade as the ship sailed away, he would have killed either himself or the captain except for his love of Mary.

Later John managed to join the crew of a slave trade ship, the brutal traffic he so much regretted in later years. This life blotted out his early religious training and led him

into bad behavior. Finally, though, when a fierce March storm one night in 1748 threatened to sink his ship, he prayed for the first time in years. And for the rest of his life he regarded every March 21 as the anniversary of his conversion. Relapses occurred, but after a serious illness he committed himself to God, returned to England, and married Mary in 1750.

John worked for a while in civil service in the region of Yorkshire. But soon he became popular as a lay preacher, developing friendships with George Whitefield and John Wesley, and began to consider the ministry. Although he studied biblical languages and theology privately, he received ordination in the Church of England only after completing his autobiography, *Authentic Narrative*, in 1764, an account that caused influential religious leaders to recognize his spiritual commitment. The book was soon translated into several languages.

John's principal sponsor for priesthood, Lord William Dartmouth, helped arrange the station for John in Olney,

and for the next sixteen years he lived in the vicarage and preached at St. Peter's and St. Paul's and in surrounding parishes. His religious devotion, remarkable personal history, and natural poetic skills gave John the gifts and preparation for writing hymns—especially one great hymn—but he needed a circumstance to prompt him. That came in 1767 when William Cowper moved to Olney.

William was one of England's fine eighteenth-century poets, producing *The Task* (1784) and translations of Homer. He received an excellent literary education at Westminster School in London and, at his father's wish, studied for the bar. But he lived an often-miserable life. Depression, his distaste for the law, poverty, and an ill-fated romance with his cousin Theodora Cowper ruined any chances of happiness. More than once he attempted suicide.

During this trauma William found relief in the home of friends first made in Huntingdon—Morley and Mary Unwin, a religious and wealthy couple. When Morley died from a fall from his horse in April of 1767, Mary moved to

Olney with her daughter Susanna to be near the renowned preacher John Newton. In fact, only an orchard stood between the rear yard of their house, Orchard Side, and John's vicarage. Soon, William also came to Olney and moved in with them. The two poets became close friends, and by 1771 they were collaborating on what became one of England's most successful hymnals, *The Olney Hymns.*

On a bright June afternoon we stroll with Elizabeth Knight in the garden of Orchard Side, now the Cowper & Newton museum, where she has been curator for more than thirty years. Nestled in the rows of flowers is an odd little summerhouse in which William gazed through its side and rear windows. Here he wrote most of the hymns in his part of the collection. After another lapse into depression, he wrote few others, but by that time he had composed his great hymns, "There is a Fountain" and "God Moves in a Mysterious Way."

Leaving the Orchard Side garden, we walk through the site of the original orchard, to the back of the two-story brick vicarage, and look up to the last dormer window on the top right. Here, in this room, during the last two weeks of December 1772, John Newton wrote "Amazing Grace."

In his book *Amazing Grace: The Story of America's Most Beloved Hymn* (Harper Collins, 2002), music historian Steve Turner records that John routinely wrote hymns to accompany his sermons and composed "Amazing Grace" in preparation for a New Year's Day sermon on January 1, 1773. He also observes that the words of the hymn evidently paraphrase entries from John's notebook. For example, the entry "Millions of unseen dangers" is rendered "through many dangers, toils, and snares" in the song. Turner gives these illustrations of Newton's use of the Scriptures in the hymn:

Newton embroidered biblical phrases and allusions into all his writing.

The image of being lost and found alludes to the parable of the prodigal son, where the father is quoted as saying in Luke 15:24,

*"For this my son was dead, and is alive again;
he was lost, and is found."*

*His confession of wretchedness may have been drawn
from Paul's exclamation in Rom. 7:24,
"O wretched man that I am!
Who shall deliver me from the body of this death?"*

*The contrast of blindness and sight refers directly
to John 9:25, when a man healed by Jesus says,
"One thing I know, that, whereas I was blind,
now I see."*

*Newton had used this phrase in his diary
during his seafaring days when he wrote on
August 9, 1752,*

*"The reason [for God's mercy] is unknown to
me, but one thing I know, that whereas
I was blind, now I see."*

Turner observes that this day of the introduction
of "Amazing Grace," in Lord Dartmouth's Great House in
Olney, was also the last that the despondent William Cowper
came to church.

LOST & FOUND

John and William published *The Olney Hymns* in 1779. The following year, 1880, William Cowper died, and John accepted a pulpit position at St. Mary Woolnoth Church in London. Audiences continued large here as well. Visitors today can pass through a wrought-iron gate and coffee shop at the entrance, walk through the church doors into the sanctuary, and view the ornate pulpit where the slave-trader turned preacher delivered sermons for the next twenty-seven years, becoming a major figure in the evangelical portion of the Anglican Church. He died on December 21, 1807, and was buried with Mary at St. Mary Woolchurch in London. They were re-interred at the Church of St. Peter and St. Paul in Olney in 1893. And he is primarily remembered for these touching words:

Amazing Grace *(1772)*
Ephesians 2:8-9

Amazing grace! How sweet the sound
That saved a wretch like me!
I once was lost, but now am found;
Was blind, but now I see.

'Twas grace that taught my heart to fear,
And grace my fears relieved;
How precious did that grace appear
The hour I first believed!

The Lord has promised good to me,
His Word my hope secures;
He will my Shield and Portion be,
As long as life endures.

The earth shall soon dissolve like snow,
The sun forbear to shine;
But God, who called me here below,
Will be forever mine.

A SINNER FINDS A HIDING PLACE

The county of Devon, on England's South West Peninsula, separates the Bristol Channel from the English Channel. It is the last county before Cornwall and a place appropriately known as Land's End, because after that there is only the vast Atlantic.

This is open country: space, hills, rock cliffs, and small parish villages. Today we are driving to Broadhembury, home of Augustus Toplady (1740–1778), writer of "Rock of Ages." To get there we obediently follow the commands of the cheerful GPS voice down a one-car-wide road closed in by a tunnel of six-foot hedgerows. I wonder what we will do if we meet someone coming toward us, but British drivers manage that problem with little trouble by just scooting slightly to the left off the paved road to make room for the cars to pass each other.

When we finally exit the hedgerows, we enter a town of very pricey thatched-roof houses, a stately thirteenth-century church, a single inn proudly displaying the sign of the Red Lion, and a happy-looking and quite comfortable population just a shade under seven hundred. The exquisitely

lovely English landscape now attracts people who blend with it and can afford expensive homes in a countryside setting.

During the last century, Broadhembury has enjoyed the patronage of the family of business magnate Julius Drewe, who bought most of the depression-ravaged village in 1903. According to village historian Christine Dunford, however, the first member of the Drewe family in possession of Broadhembury purchased it in 1595 from none other than Henry, the Earl of Southampton, the patron of Shakespeare addressed in his sonnets. So when Augustus became vicar of St. Andrews church in 1768 (the thirty-fourth vicar since 1311), he became part of a long local and church history.

We meet Christine at the church, where thousands of hymns, including some composed by Augustus, have echoed over eight hundred years. Inscriptions on the walls contain both solemn remembrances and charming requests. Alongside memorials that tell of village soldiers lost in wars, an ancient plaque records that in 1725:

A Person unknown, gave the Inter.ft
of Ten Pounds p.r Ann: to poor Labourers
receiving no monthly pay

And a much more contemporary paper note tacked to the front door reads this way:

Welcome to St. Andrews Church, Broadhembury.
Please close the door on entering and leaving.
Birds fly in the Church and cannot get out.
Thank You.
Have a safe journey home.

Augustus Toplady was born on November 4, 1740, and educated at Westminster School in London and at Trinity College, Dublin. Converted by a sermon delivered in a barn in Ireland in 1755, he became curate at Blagdon, Somersetshire, in 1762. Ordained an Anglican priest two years later, he served in Somerset and Devon villages before coming to Broadhembury.

Augustus was a spiritual preacher, if maybe a bit of a loner. His positive traits, however, were partially offset by his extremely bitter controversy with John Wesley, during which Augustus held rigidly to his Calvinistic beliefs and bitterly attacked the Methodist leader up to the very end of Augustus's life in London in 1778 at age thirty-eight.

Sometime during the Blagdon years, Augustus wrote "Rock of Ages," one of the most beloved of all Christian hymns. The circumstances of his writing it are legendary, whether or not the legend is true, so we drive out to Cheddar Gorge to see the rock that he immortalized in his hymn.

Cheddar Gorge is one of the most scenic spots in western England, part of Somerset's Burington Combe area.

A SINNER FINDS A HIDING PLACE

As we drive through its floor, between rock walls hundreds of feet high, we see parties of rock climbers and small herds of mountain goats perched above us.

Slanting down one of the rock cliffs is a long, straight crevice, maybe a hundred feet high. Here, the story goes, Augustus found cover when he and his horse were caught in a violent rain storm. Always seeking spiritual parallels, he imagined the sheltering cleft as a figure of the saving Christ and conceived the idea for a hymn. Needing some paper on which to write it, he looked around and found a playing card left by a previous visitor probably less inclined toward religion. It was all he had, so he composed his poem on it. A blue highlighted inscription on the face of the cliff testifies to this account. Across the road, a sign announces the date of the next annual Rock of Ages service.

Apparently there's no documentation for this story, and most sources doubt it. Whatever the case, many believers have found the words of "Rock of Ages" to be the most moving expression in English hymns of the sinner's plea for salvation by Christ's blood.

The first verse appeals for shelter in Christ, the Rock (cf. 1 Corinthians 10:4), whose body was "cleft," giving blood and water (John 19:34). The second and third verses emphasize that this salvation is by grace, not by any labor, zeal, repenting tears, or price offered by the sinner (cf. Ephesians 2:8–9). In theme, then, it resembles John Newton's hymn "Amazing Grace."

Augustus included "Rock of Ages" in his *Psalms and Hymns for Public and Private Worship* of 1776, published the year of the American Revolution. Altogether he wrote about 130 hymns, including this one, loved and sung ever since by millions.

SUNSET AT EVENTIDE

On the coast of Devon lies Lower Brixham, an ancient fishing village built on the inlet known as Torbay. It offers one of England's most beautiful settings, especially as seen from the rocks on the shore below the hotel called Berry Head. Brilliant sunshine glitters like diamonds across azure blue calm water and gorgeous balls of pink flowers or delicate white ones are set against dark green leaves. In the town, pastel-colored houses perch on terraces overlooking the harbor, mirrored in the glass-top water. The picturesque beauty seems as lasting as an oil painting. But, as John Keats reminds us in "Ode to Melancholy," beauty is at its peak when just on the verge of leaving.

Transience and fading beauty are especially evident in Torbay's sunsets. Just before it disappears, an orange sun is caught between a dark horizontal cloud and the blackened shore across the bay. As it silently sets, the glow gradually fades and darkness comes. For twenty-seven years, Henry Lyte, priest of All-Saints Church in Brixham, watched that sunset, and in September of 1847 he knew what it predicted for him. Faced with inevitable change, sad decay, and encroaching blindness, he prayed to Him who abides.

Henry Francis Lyte was born in Scotland to a military officer and his wife. The family moved to Ireland during the Napoleonic wars, and by the time he was nine Henry was alone. Befriended by the first of several benefactors, he eventually was admitted to Trinity College to study ministry. While there he demonstrated not only excellent scholarship and a lovable personality, but also notable ability as a poet. After receiving his degree of master of arts, Henry served churches in Taghman and then Cornwall, England, where he married Anne Maxwell.

In 1823 Henry became rector of the church in Lower Brixham, where he was beloved by the Devon fishermen's families whom he and Anne served. His church was full on Sundays, and he always made sure that a Bible was on any boat that left the harbor. He also composed several hymns, including "Jesus, I My Cross Have Taken" and "Praise, My Soul, the King of Heaven." Through the generosity of another benefactor, they lived in unexpectedly fine surroundings at Berry Head, a former hospital built for the Napoleonic wars that overlooked Torbay. His frail health began to deteriorate with tuberculosis, however, and he began spending winters in the warmer climate of the French Riviera.

In the fall of 1847 Henry planned to leave for Rome. On Sunday, September 4, he painfully climbed into his pulpit in All-Saints, probably knowing that this could be his last sermon for the humble people of Brixham. Later that afternoon he walked the familiar shore at Berry Head, gazing fondly at the town and at the quiet bay he had seen almost daily for nearly thirty years. At last, he returned to his room and penned the hymn that expressed his most fervent prayer as evening began to close over him. Based on Luke 24:29, it began . . .

Abide with me; fast falls the eventide;
The darkness deepens; Lord, with me abide.
When other helpers fail and comforts flee,
Help of the helpless, O abide with me.

A few days later Henry left Lower Brixham, crossed the choppy English Channel, and headed toward Rome. He carried his new hymn with him and continued to revise it. But in Nice, France, his weary lungs succumbed to the racking tuberculosis, and he died at the Hotel de Angleterre, attended by a minister also staying there. Henry was buried at Nice in the English Cemetery of the Holy Trinity Church. His last and most enduring song was sent back to Lower Brixham and given to his son-in-law, and "Abide with Me" was sung at his memorial service in All-Saints.

Today nets and fishing gear symbolic of the parishioners Henry served hang in the vestry of the large church later built in Brixham. His hymn, a favorite of Mahatma Gandhi and King George V, is sung throughout the world by believers who seek the Lord's abiding presence, especially at eventide.

23

Llanlleonfel church in the Irfon Valley of Wales—a heavy, gray-stone building at the top of a secluded hill—dreams quietly of its past. Narrow loophole windows of leaden glass peer down at us as we stroll solemnly through the churchyard filled with lichen-covered tombstones centuries old. Quiet reflection reigns here now.

On April 8, 1749, though, the church originally standing here was filled with eager anticipation as Charles Wesley waited for Miss Sarah Gwynne to walk from nearby Garth House along the path up that hill to Llanlleonfel to be his bride. A restless, joyful yearning would characterize Charles all of his life, and it would become a major theme in the some forty-five hundred published works that place him at the front of a long list of British hymnwriters.

Born the eighteenth child of a minister, Charles followed throughout his life the influence of his older brother, John. In 1726 he joined John as a student at Christ Church, Oxford, to prepare to preach. Here they led a group of spiritually committed young men whose discipline was so strict that their fellow students taunted them with such names as Bible Moths, the Holy Club, and, finally,

Methodists. Thus the two brothers unwittingly began a major Protestant denomination. John later attended Oxford's Lincoln College. We visit his rooms, now preserved for visitors.

Ordained an Anglican priest in 1735, Charles let his optimistic spirit lead him into joining John for a mission trip to Georgia in the American colonies, where he became secretary to General James Oglethorpe. But he was unsuited for the work; so in poor health and restless, he returned to Britain the next year. There, in 1738, following an intense religious conversion, he began a decade of itinerant evangelical preaching throughout England, ever wandering in search of spiritual fulfillment.

John returned from America and established himself in Bristol as the powerful and determined leader of the evangelical Methodist movement. After Charles married Sarah, he finally settled down near his brother, living from 1749 to 1771 in a house near John's meeting center, called the New Room, to support his work there.

Arriving at the New Room, we enter from the rear. At the far end, two white pulpits, one stacked above and behind the other, all trimmed in perfect symmetry, gleam through the beams of sunlight streaming from a large octagonal skylight in the ceiling. On the floor of the aged auditorium, and in the

balconies that surround it on the side and rear walls, are dark wooden pews with straight backs. At first we imagine these seats filled with worshippers listening to John preaching from the pulpit, but then a rather intimidating sign informs us that "This block of pews has nothing to do with John Wesley!" It seems that the rigorous leader favored much more Spartan, plain backless benches of the kind lining the walls today.

Wandering up the creaking stairs and past the great pulpits, we enter the Preacher's Room. Now a museum containing memorabilia of the Wesleys and their contemporary ministers, it houses among other things a chair carved from a tree trunk, which once served Bible commentator Adam Clarke. We end our stay at the New Room outside in the courtyard where a statue of Charles, one arm raised in kindly appeal, bears the inscription "Let Me Commend My Savior to You."

We find Charles' house a few blocks away, but it's closed to the public except for specially arranged tours. It was here in this narrow red brick structure that Charles lived with

Sarah and their three children and composed hundreds of his famous hymns.

After their years in Bristol, the Wesley brothers finally moved to London and to the Wesley Chapel, center of their work for the rest of their lives. This Georgian-style church, John's adjacent house and burial place, and nearby Bunhill Fields cemetery—site of the graves of Isaac Watts and other hymn writers—are a mecca for devotees of the Wesleys. The present sanctuary and pulpit are far more elaborate than the New Room's and are in marked contrast to John's simple wooden pulpit on display in the museum downstairs.

At Wesley Chapel we encounter many more fellow visitors than in Bristol, but we are fortunate enough to receive a private tour of John's house led by an enthusiastic and kind volunteer. He shows us a small room where John went to pray mornings at four o'clock before his busy day began. Ironically, Charles' London house—home of one of England's most treasured preachers—has since been converted into a pub.

Charles, like his brother John, was himself a preacher, but during these years his major contribution to Christianity was his prolific output of powerful and touching hymns, centering on the grace of Christ and urging us to recognize and joyfully seek it. He produced several thousand songs, and many have become the most familiar and frequently used in Britain and America. Beloved for their happy, rejoicing themes, they include "A Charge to Keep I Have," "Christ the Lord Is Risen Today," "Jesus, Lover of My Soul," the carol "Hark! the Herald Angels Sing," and finally, "Love Divine, All Love Excelling," a hymn urging Christ to visit us, indicative of Charles' joyful yearning.

A WEDDING PRAYER

One morning in the fall of 1800, Dorothy Wordsworth (1771–1855), who lived near the village of Grasmere in the Lake District of England with her famous brother William, wrote this account:

> A fine October morning—sat in the house working
> all the morning. Wm composing—Sally Ashburner
> learning to mark. After Dinner we walked up
> Greenhead Gill in search of a sheepfold. We went by
> Mr. Oliff's & through his woods. It was a delightful day
> & the views looked excessively cheerful & beautiful . . .
> The colours of the mountains soft & rich, with orange
> fern—The Cattle pasturing upon the hill-tops.
> Kites sailing as in the sky above our heads—
> Sheep bleating & in lines & chains & patterns
> scattered over the mountains.

The Lake District is one of the world's most scenic places. Thousands come each summer to walk the trails, view the low ranges of mountains, and ponder the sky as it changes from blue to misty gray.

Tucked in a nook of this idyllic setting, a few miles from the town of Ambleside on Lake Windemere and down a quiet winding road, is the community of Brathay. The center of activity here for a century and a half or so has been Holy Trinity Church. It sits on a hill so limited in space that the church had to be positioned North/South instead of the traditional East/West. (The graves, though, are arranged traditionally: laity facing east and clergy west.) A tall, ivy-covered tower houses the entrance, and inside an especially fine arched wooden ceiling assures beautiful acoustics for church music.

We are met here today by Janet Martindale, a cheerful and impressive lady who knows nearly all things Ambleside

DOROTHY FRANCES BLOMFIELD GURNEY   31

and Brathay. She greets us with her daughter, Emma Jane, a quiet and energetic young woman who guides visitors around the Lake District and is soon to become church warden. Janet quickly gives us a packet of articles and pictures carefully collected since my call from the States a few weeks before. They tell about the church and especially the Lake District's most famous Christian hymn, the product of another Dorothy: "O Perfect Love"—probably the most often used of English wedding songs.

We have the church to ourselves, so Janet and Emma Jane tell us the story.

It happened in the winter of 1883, when Miss Katherine Blomfield and her family from London were visiting Ambleside at Howsley Cottage and planning her wedding to prominent Brathay surgeon Hugh Redmayne on January 25, just three weeks away. She still needed a song for her wedding and was a tad nervous, but she was attracted

by a hymn entitled "Strength and Stay." (Janet shows us a copy.) The original lyrics were written in Latin in the fourth century by St. Ambrose (c. 340–397), but recently they had been translated into English by John Ellerton (1826–1893) and F.J.A. Hort (1828–1892). Ambrose and John, though, had not been writing a song for a wedding. But, it was really the song's tune, supplied by John Dykes (1823–1876), that Katherine really wanted, and now wanted badly.

The frustrated bride-to-be turned to her older sister, Dorothy, 25, who was known for her poetry, and said, "What's the use of a sister who composes poetry if she cannot write new words to a favorite tune? I would like to use this tune at my wedding."

What happened next is one of Britain's favorite hymn stories. Dorothy replied that if everyone would leave her alone, she would see what she could do. She then picked up the song and retired to the cottage library. Thirty minutes

A WEDDING PRAYER

later (some say fifteen) she emerged with the words now famous. Like those of Ambrose, they constitute a prayer, this one for the young couple. God is addressed with the names "perfect Love" and "perfect Life" and asked to grant them love (verse 1); faith, hope, endurance, and trust (verse 2); and joy, peace, and a final place in heaven (verse 3). A few isolated phrases bear a justifiable resemblance to Ellerton's translation.

Six years later, in 1889, Dorothy's hastily written song soared in popularity. First it was placed in the popular hymnal *Hymns Ancient and Modern.* Then it enjoyed the best fortune a British wedding hymn could have: Queen Victoria's granddaughter, Princess Louise of Wales, daughter of King Edward VII and sister of King George V, chose "O Perfect Love" for her wedding to Alexander William George Duff, first Duke of Fife, at Buckingham Palace. She also asked famous composer Joseph Barnaby for a fresh tune, and he wrote "Sandringham," named after the palace where the princess had been brought up. "O Perfect Love" soon became the choice of brides-to-be in Britain and America and held its place for the next half century.

Dorothy never exercised copyright for the hymn, though it might have brought her considerable returns. She later married Gerald Gurney, and later on they were received into the Roman Catholic Church. She died in 1932 and enjoys the reputation of having remained the cheerful, helpful lady she was to her sister. In 1986 one of her descendants, Judith Gurney, was married in Brathay church. The guests sang "O Perfect Love."

33

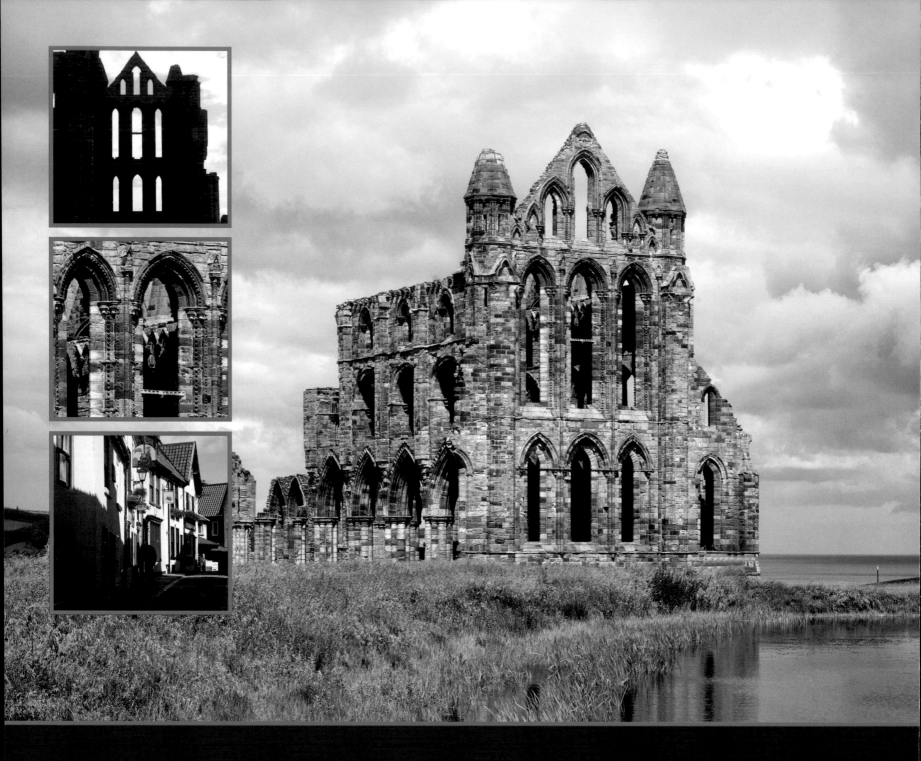

HYMNS OF A SHY HERDSMAN

ven from a distance, the skeleton of the Abbey is haunting, etched against the gray clouds of an overcast sky and the dark blue of the level sea. When I approach it, looking from the east at its most intact side with the sea beyond, I watch as the sun appears and lightens it or goes behind the clouds, throwing its stones into shadow.

Viewed from the south, the ruined arches and columns look like bones, all that was left after Henry VIII's men savaged it. Still, they stand in perfect, orderly rows, like quiet monks at service, white clouds and light blue sky now behind them, the green grass a carpet where the stone floor used to be.

Whitby Abbey stands on the east cliff of north Yorkshire, overlooking the North Sea. It was founded by Oswy, Anglo-Saxon king of Northumbria, in 657. He named Lady Hilda, niece of the first Christian king of Northumbria, as abbess. According to the monk historian named Bede

(c. 657–680), it was during her tenure that the first hymn was written in English by a herdsman named Caedmon.

The town of Whitby features fleets of fishing boats, twisting streets lined with small shops displaying pies, cakes trimmed with brightly colored icing, souvenirs, and, during the summer, whatever else will attract visitors come to see the Abbey. During the winter the town is given over to cold winds, empty lanes, and patient survival.

From town level we walk up a set of steep curving steps past a monument to Caedmon, which proclaims him

The Father of English Sacred Song

A religious party speaking what sounds like Dutch gathers around their guide. A group of school children chatter excitedly as they scamper in a ragged row across the grass under the arches. Each wears a large backpack. Even on this late June day they've been dressed wisely by their mothers in long pants, sweaters, and hats against the north wind off the sea. For now the air is calm, fresh, and cool, but not biting.

CAEDMON'S HYMN

(late seventh century)

Genesis 1:1

Original Northumbrian Version

Nu we sculon herigean heofonrices weard,
Meotodes meahte ond his modgeþance,
Weorc wuldorfæder, swa he wundra gehwæs,
Ece drihten, or onstealde.
He ærest sceop eorðan bearnum
heofon to hrofe, halig scyppend;
Þa middangeard moncynnes weard,
ece drihten, æfter teode
firum foldan, frea ælmihtig.

Modern English Version

Now [we] must honour the guardian of heaven,
the might of the architect, and his purpose,
the work of the father of glory — as he,
the eternal lord, established the beginning
of wonders. He, the holy creator,
first created heaven as a roof for the children of men.
Then the guardian of mankind, the eternal lord,
the lord almighty, afterwards appointed
the middle earth, the lands, for men.

We go to the east side of the Abbey to view it over a long reflecting pool. Nearby a sunken trench holds a row of relic stones taken from the structure. For centuries it was scoured by the locals for building materials. I stare at it as I listen to the audio recording telling Caedmon's story.

The account comes from the pages of Bede's *Historia Ecclesiastica Gentis Anglorum (Ecclesiastical History of the English People)*, the earliest and most authentic record of ancient England, finished in 731.

Caedmon was a shy man, and he was embarrassed at celebrations when, according to custom, a harp was passed around and each person took a turn singing for the entertainment of the group. His problem was that he could not sing, so before the harp would get to him he would make some excuse and leave.

One night after Caedmon had slipped out this way and gone to feed his animals, he fell asleep and had a dream. A man appeared and told him to sing a song about "the beginning of created things." Caedmon tried to avoid singing, but the man would not let him, and suddenly this common herdsman found himself able to compose a poem. After waking the next day he remembered the dream, including the words of his poem, and was even able to add to it.

When Hilda heard what had happened to Caedmon, she decided the incident was a gift from God, and as a test she ordered him to compose a poem about "a passage of sacred history or doctrine." The next day he returned with his second poem, and Hilda ordered that he take vows as a monk and be taught further sacred stories and doctrines. Caedmon found that after each lesson he could turn it into beautiful poetry. He continued this service until his peaceful death in 680.

Caedmon's hymn written in Bede's history, in Anglo-Saxon or Old English, may well be the oldest surviving English poem. Almost certainly it is the oldest English hymn, the first of many over the centuries leading to the great hymns whose stories are recorded in this book.

THIS MOUNT
WAS A
FAVOURITE RETIREMENT
OF THE LATE
ISAAC WATTS D.D.

A DISSENTER'S GIFT OF HIMSELF

The port city of Southampton on the southern coast of England has been the final point of departure for thousands of hopeful or desperate people. The winds were cool the late fall day in 1620 when the *Mayflower* sailed and cool, too, on April 10, 1912, when the *Titanic* grandly steamed out.

On this summer day, though, the salty air is warm as we stroll toward the town park. In the center flowers surround the statue of this sea city's most famous citizen, but one who never sailed anywhere or even traveled much farther than London. Four times each day, from the tower of the town hall that we see from the park, the notes of "O God, Our Help in Ages Past" float over the image of its composer, Isaac Watts, often called "the father of English hymnody."

Isaac's father certainly never expected any honor for his family from Southampton. Three times he was imprisoned as a Dissenting preacher by being locked in the city gaol, a building ironically called God's House that still stands by the Old South Gate. His Above Bar Congregational Church remained until the mid-twentieth century.

The oldest child of eight, Isaac was brilliant from the first but neither healthy nor attractive. He stood five feet tall, with a head that was too large for his body. Once when he asked a girl to marry him, she turned him down, saying that while she could love the jewel she could never love the case it came in.

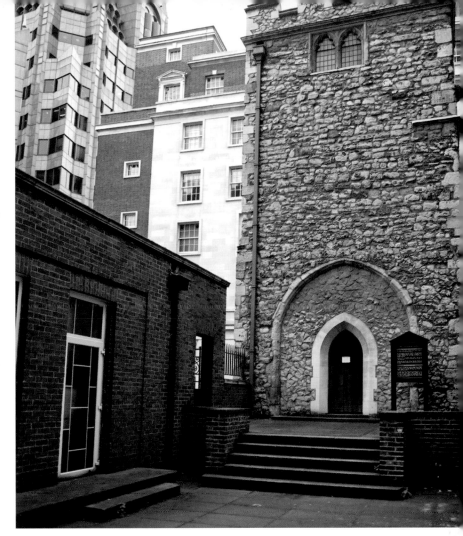

Isaac was a poetic progeny all his life. His co-pastor, Samuel Price, told the story of how one Sunday morning when he was a young man, Isaac complained to his father about the singing at Southampton's Above Bar Church. So his father sharply challenged Isaac to improve on it. In response, Isaac produced the first in a body of hymns that not only became the finest yet written but broke the long-standing hymn tradition of restricting lyrics to poetic versions of the Scriptures, principally the Psalms. Instead, Isaac wrote his own words, expressing his personal spiritual and emotional feelings. After that a flood of glorious musical poetry flowed, not only from Isaac Watts, but from the hearts and pens of the great hymnwriters who followed him.

Isaac was also denied entrance to university because of his independent beliefs. So he studied instead with renowned Dissenting teacher Thomas Rowe of Stoke Newington, a village near London. Ultimately he became pastor of the Mark Lane church in the city and also preached at All Hallows Staining. Its tower, built around 1320, is all that remains of that church today.

An unidentified major illness afflicted Isaac all of his life, however, and often interrupted his ministry. But it also resulted in a lifetime living arrangement allowing him two achievements. First, he became the most brilliant independent scholar and theologian of his day, producing a book on logic used at Oxford University for a hundred years. Second, and even more important he, along with Charles Wesley, achieved the plateau of Britain's two greatest hymnwriters.

In 1712 Sir Thomas and Lady Mary Abney, aristocratic members at Mark Lane, invited Isaac to stay a week at their home at Theobalds in Hertfordshire to help

forward his recovery. That visit evolved into a permanent home for Isaac at Theobalds, at their house in London, and later at the manor house of their large country estate at Abney Park in Stoke Newington. Isaac, who never married, happily lived at Abney Park from 1736 until his death, drawing inspiration from the flocks of herons on the lake island and from the natural beauty of the scenic retreat.

On a pedestal in a discontinued cemetery in Stoke Newington stands a statue of a small man holding a harp. A fence of black wrought-iron spears provides some sort of protection. Otherwise the grounds and most of the graves are overgrown, all but one covered with vines, the whole threatened by encroaching inferior wild trees. The cemetery was abandoned in the 1930s because of inferior burial practices. Nearby is a ruined chapel, defaced with graffiti, the only remaining structure of Abney Park. The manor house is gone. Isaac's statue presides over this scene of bygone luxury and serenity. His body lies in a tomb in Bunhill Fields Cemetery in London, also the burial place of John Bunyan,

A DISSENTER'S GIFT OF HIMSELF

novelist Daniel Defoe, and a host of literary and musical celebrities.

By the time of his death in 1748, Isaac had written about 750 hymns, including "Come We That Love the Lord"; "Alas! and Did My Saviour Bleed?"; "Am I a Soldier of the Cross?"; "How Shall the Young Secure Their Hearts?"; "I'm Not Ashamed to Own My Lord"; "The Lord My Shepherd Is"; and "This Is the Day the Lord Hath Made." But of all his hymns, three are among the most beloved and familiar of Christian hymns: "O God, Our Help in Ages Past"; "Joy to the World!"; and the hymn pronounced by nineteenth-century writer and critic Matthew Arnold to be the greatest hymn ever written in English, "When I Survey the Wondrous Cross."

The persona or speaker in this beloved hymn focuses on his own unworthiness in contrast to the holiness and worthiness of Christ in His death on the cross, a reflection of Galatians 6:14. Witnessing the crucifixion of Christ, the speaker joins the apostle Paul, who wrote Galatians, in rejecting any worldly possession, status, or personal pride (Paul called it "rubbish"), desiring only His saving blood (verses 1 and 2). He marvels at the blend of sorrow and love in that blood (verse 3), and in response, he declares himself dead to the world (verse 4). The simile in the line "His dying crimson, like a robe, / Spreads o'er His body on the tree" is among the finest in English poetry.

Realizing the incomparable gift that Christ has made for him, the speaker recognizes that, even if he possessed all of nature, it would be "far too small" a present to offer in return (verse 5). Rather, the "amazing" love of Christ demands, not a gift *from* himself, but the gift *of* himself: "my soul, my life, my all."

HERE'S MY HEART

Anyone riding down St. Andrews Street in Cambridge will easily spot Stoneyard Baptist Church. The tall façade with ornate glass windows, three arched entrances, and soaring bell tower is covered with hundreds of unfinished gray stones. Even the church's coffee shop to the right of the tower has an identical décor and is named LivingStones. Probably this site was once that of a quarry or place of a business dealing in stones, but when Robert Robinson (1735–1790) came here to preach in 1761, the church was already named Stoneyard Baptist Chapel.

We reach the sanctuary from an entrance off the coffee shop, which still has wooden scrolling and the words "Sunday School Lecture Hall 1889." The auditorium inside is a busy mix of old and new and a contrast to the Anglican churches we have been visiting. In spite of the church's name, there are no stone columns and arches here. Instead our attention is instantly drawn to the startling Tudor-style ceiling where dark timbers in elaborate patterns crisscross the whole against a white background. This geometric design dominates the room.

The pews on the floor curve around the altar area, and a balcony stretches around the sides and back. At the front handsome, distinctly Protestant woodwork forms a wide, commanding, raised pulpit reached on each side by steps with steel railings. On the floor in front of the pulpit are seven carved chairs, the central one grander and more ornate, standing behind an unusually large, plain communion table.

With the exception of the ceiling, this is the traditional view one might expect in a British Baptist church. But here, as in most Protestant auditoriums during the last quarter century, a new element has entered.

Between the communion table and the audience stands a surprisingly large and ornate portable speaker's stand equipped with a microphone. It has evidently been left there from an informal presentation made sometime between our visit and the preceding Sunday service. But maybe it was used even then. Today's preachers often prefer to step down to this kind of podium to get physically and psychologically closer to their more relaxed and sometimes smaller audiences.

Most innovative of all, a large white projection screen has been inserted behind the formal, commanding pulpit,

blocking the view of the stained-glass window behind. This intruder is portable and could be removed any time, I guess, but I still get the sense that twenty-first-century technology has wedged itself into hundreds of years of British tradition since the days of Robert Robinson.

Robert's debt-ridden father died while the boy was still very young, and he was apprenticed to a hairdresser. His companions were rough, but he heard evangelical preachers, especially George Whitefield, and eventually was converted and began preaching, first in the Methodist and then in the independent Baptist tradition. He was invited to serve on a trial basis at Stoneyard Baptist Chapel in 1759. There were only thirty-four members, and his salary was less than four pounds for six months, but he stayed. His preaching helped build the church membership in a dozen years to over five hundred. He preached through the week in nearby villages consisting of some fifty parishes, and was accepted by the Cambridge University community as well. He preached at Stoneyard Baptist the rest of his life.

Robert was a Dissenter and a nonconformist throughout his entire preaching career, organizing relief for Dissenter ministers and children, combating slavery, and even opposing taxation practices against the American colonies in 1775. He advocated preaching to the illiterate and to common audiences, and he especially opposed any pressure to violate conscience or to override the Scriptures. He died in his bed in June 1790.

Robert wrote several hymns, including "Come, Thou Fount of Every Blessing," composed for the conclusion of a sermon in 1758. Especially popular in America today, it is a hymn of praise to God for His grace and a petition that a sense of God's help and goodness will hold the pilgrim faithful until he reaches home. An especially notable phrase in the hymn is in the second verse: "Here I raise my Ebenezer: Hither by Thy help I've come." Ebenezer means "stone of help" and is an allusion to 1 Samuel 7:12 in which Samuel erected a stone between Mizpah and Shen and named it Ebenezer, saying, "Thus far has the Lord helped us," and intimating that He will surely help us in the way ahead.

FOUNTAIN OF BLESSINGS

ourton-on-the-Water, one of the loveliest villages in the Cotswolds and all of England, has its name from the clear, wide stream that gently meanders through the length of the town, running through a channel between stone walls built centuries ago. Every so often arched walkways span the water, allowing easy access to either side and a photo spot for locals in for the day or visitors from the Orient on an England trip-of-a-lifetime.

On both sides of the stream are walks and strips of carefully-tended turf supplied with park benches, allowing strollers to go slowly along beneath the trees and by the shops. They can sit and watch the squadrons of gliding ducks as they steer their young beneath the arches of the bridges, skillfully avoiding an occasional pet dog that splashes in and out of the water.

Along the waterway stand honey-colored buildings of the Cotswold stone that makes the region famous—shops, hotels, and occasional residences with names like the

Knightsbridge Inn and Grey Gables. One of these, situated right by a bridge, is the Old Manse Hotel. Since 1963 it has provided housing and fare for thousands of visitors, the dining room menu urging patrons, "Don't forget to look at the range of Sunday Roasts & Chef's Daily Specials featured on our blackboards before you order!"

In older centuries of England a manse was the home of a minister, and this one was built in 1718 at a cost of £350 to serve as the home for the pastor of the village Baptist church. In 1740 Benjamin Beddome (1717–1795), a Particular Baptist (one who adheres strictly to Calvinist beliefs) and hymnwriter, became that pastor, and he remained so for fifty-five years until he died.

Born on January 23, 1717, to a Baptist minister in Bristol, Benjamin became a member of the Prescott Street Baptist Church in 1739 and chose to become a preacher himself. Moving to Bourton-on-the-Water the next year, he began a successful ministry, which ultimately led to his receiving a master of arts degree from Providence College in Rhode Island. Like other ministers included in this book, he had the practice of writing hymns to be sung at the close of his sermons. A few of these were published during his lifetime, and in 1817, the one hundredth anniversary of his

birth, 830 of his hymns were published under the title *Hymns Adapted for Public Worship or Family Devotion.*

Benjamin's memorial marker is in a cemetery where many of the stones have fallen to weather and time. Most are crowded together, but Benjamin's stands separate from the others. The inscription reads,

SACRED
TO THE MEMORY OF
BENJAMIN BEDDOME
BORN 1717. DIED 1785
FOR 52 YEARS THE PASTOR OF THE
BAPTIST CHAPEL
BOURTON-ON-THE-WATER.
INTERRED NEAR THIS SPOT
WHERE THE CHAPEL FORMERLY STOOD
THE MEMORY OF THE JUST IS BLESSED
THIS STONE WAS ERECTED BY HIS
GREAT GRANDCHILDREN

The staff at the Old Manse understandably don't know much about Benjamin beyond the historical plaque on the lobby wall, which is reprinted on the menu. Standing on the little bridge outside, I reflect on how he watched this gentle, shallow stream flow by for half a century. It seems appropriate, and maybe even connected, that his most famous hymn by far, "God is the Fountain Whence," begins with the metaphor of a fountain. It shows him to be, like all of the hymnwriters whose homes we have visited, a devout, thankful, and hopeful man of faith.

49

FRAGRANCE FROM THE GARDENS OF HODNET HALL

I know a bank where the wild thyme blows,
Where oxlips and the nodding violet grows,
Quite over-canopied with luscious woodbine,
With sweet musk-roses and with eglantine.

A Midsummer Night's Dream (2.1.)

As I walk along this Shropshire garden path "over-canopied" with ancient oaks, wisteria, astrantia, rhododendron, lupins, phlox, liquid amber, and fifty other species of plants, myriad fragrances float to me on the breezes off the Main Pool below the mansion. Brushing against an elephant leaf and feeling the startled dewdrops fall on my arm, I reflect that Shakespeare could have been describing this place—the Gardens of Hodnet Hall, ancestral home of hymnist, poet, parson, and squire Reginald Heber (1783–1826).

Like Sabine Baring-Gould, (see pages 90-93), Reginald was one of those rare hymn writers born to status and wealth: the Heber family of Hodnet dates back almost to the Norman Conquest of the eleventh century. A thousand years of Heber noblemen have lived here. Today the estate's manager has invited us into the exquisite rooms where the current head of the family and his wife, Algernon and Jill Heber-Percy, now live. We admire the furnishings and greet the gentle family retriever, who evidently has free run of the house.

On an end table in one of the sitting rooms lies a leather-bound book. Inside in an even script are handwritten pages of the family journal recorded by a Heber family member in the early 1800s. I gingerly hold it and leaf through the pages. There in two-hundred-year-old ink is the record of Reginald Heber, hymnist and bishop of Calcutta.

A family that traces back nearly a millennium ultimately produced several illustrious personalities. In an adjoining room an aristocratic ancestor wearing a large powdered wig stares serenely down on me from his large illuminated portrait. It hangs over a handsome ornate table with heavy marble top beside a stand holding a globe of the earth. Reginald's portrait, smaller, hangs beside that

of his ancestor. He has curly hair and a benevolent, kindly expression. His portrait so moved poet Robert Southey that he composed a poem about it.

Hodnet Hall radiates the stately yet somehow genteelly relaxed atmosphere of the English countryside. All in all it's the most elegant home currently being lived in I've ever entered. But Reginald spent his life, not as a lord of the manor, but as a clergyman. Born April 21, 1783, in Malpas, he was the son of Reginald Heber Sr., who inherited the estate. He was educated at Brasenose College, Oxford, and elected as fellow at All Souls there.

Afterwards, in the tradition of sons born to nobility, Reginald completed a grand tour of Europe, and then he settled in Hodnet as both squire of the manor and parson. He married Amelia Shipley, daughter of an influential

churchman, who helped him advance to a high Anglican church position of his own. Their daughter Emily married Algernon Percy, ancestor of the current owner of the estate.

During these years Reginald established himself as a Romantic poet, but most importantly as a major hymnwriter. Rejecting the time's suspicion of hymns that express a composer's private religious thoughts, he wrote the lyrics that led hymn historian George Rutler to name him "the brightest and best hymn writer of recent centuries." After his death Amelia included fifty-seven of his hymns as the main part of a collection entitled *Hymns Written and Adapted to the Weekly Church Service of the Year* (1827).

Reginald's major abilities, his character, and his pleasing personality won him widespread affection. Novelist William Thackeray said of him:

The charming poet, the happy possessor of all sorts of gifts and accomplishments—birth, wit, fame, high character, competence—he was the beloved priest in his own home of Hodnet, counseling the people in their troubles, advising them in their difficulties, kneeling often at their sick beds at the hazard of his own life; where there was strife, the peacemaker, where there was want, the free giver.

Reginald's service ultimately led to his appointment as Bishop of Calcutta in 1823, in effect placing him over Anglican church affairs in India, southern Africa, and Australia. He worked very hard—too much so in the end. The heat of India was stifling, but he kept on traveling and ministering to admiring throngs of people for three years.

Finally, after a particularly hard day on April 3, 1826, he plunged alone into a large bath for relief, evidently suffered an attack of apoplexy, and was discovered by his servant a half hour later at the bottom of the pool. He was forty-three years old.

I continue my stroll through the gardens. A gnarled tree bordered by green-leafed plants and red spires of flowers frames a manicured lawn. Water lilies so thick they hide the water grow on a quiet pool. A stone cherub shaded by evergreens rises modestly out of a rich bank of light green foliage. The focal point is the Main Pool, its borders undulating through banks edged by weeping willows and flowering plants. It lies before the front of the mansion on a distant hill.

Walking up the incline toward the highest part of the gardens, I follow a shaded path threading quietly through a misty maze of ferns, evergreens, and fairy-like, twisted tree-trunks up a flight of aged stone steps. At the top, hidden in the foliage and sheltered by a vine-covered conical roof, sits a small octagonal hut overlooking the gardens and pools below. I sit on the bench inside and look out, savoring the quiet and the cool, fragrant air. Here, in this secluded place, Reginald would sit to meditate and compose in the years between 1807 and 1823. Drawing peace and inspiration from the luscious, green scene below him, he wrote his spiritual songs, including his most beloved hymn.

"Holy, Holy, Holy" is based on Revelation 4:8–11, where God is worshiped by the four living creatures and by the twenty-four elders, who cast their crowns before His throne. The phrase "Early in the morning our song shall rise to Thee" perhaps reflects Reginald's personal devotions in the dawn hours spent in Hodnet Gardens.

Reginald wrote "Holy, Holy, Holy" for Trinity Sunday, which occurs eight weeks after Easter in the Anglican calendar. His original verses focus on the doctrine of the Trinity of the Father, Son, and Holy Spirit. (That doctrine was a focus of the religious council of Nicea held in AD 325; John Dykes named his 1861 tune for the hymn "Nicea.")

Interestingly, later religious groups sensitive to controversies over the concept of the Trinity altered Reginald's phrase in verses 1 and 4—"God in Three persons, blessed Trinity"—changing it to "God over all, and blest eternally."

Alfred Lord Tennyson (1809-1892), Poet Laureate of England, proclaimed "Holy, Holy, Holy" "the world's greatest hymn." The homage is a tribute to a man born to privilege who used his station for sacrificial service and a brilliant hymnal contribution.

AWAKE, MY SOUL!

As I watch from the steps leading up to the chapel, two senior student boys in their late teens cross the empty courtyard of Winchester College toward me. Both wear black pants and a solid light blue shirt, but the one on the left is also casually wearing his unbuttoned black school robe. Both have their heads bowed in conversation, and each has his right hand in his pants pocket and papers or a book in his left. This scene has been repeated here every day for more than six hundred years. Winchester is the oldest such school in England and in some particulars the model for such elite English boys' schools as Eton and Westminster.

A very pleasant feature of our visit here is that we are about the only visitors today, or at least we don't see others, and we get the feeling that most days there are few. There is little or no adjustment here for the general public, and we have a corresponding sense of how special it is to be here.

Winchester College was begun in 1382 by William Wykham, wealthy bishop of Winchester and England's lord

chancellor, primarily to educate poor boys. The first year it admitted seventy, as well as sixteen Choristers and ten paying students called Commoners. I notice that one of the pubs in the quiet town is the Wykham Arms. It is near Cornflowers, the college gift shop with the light blue doors.

We are met at the guardhouse by Susanna Foster, the college archivist, a pleasant young woman in jeans who is both helpful and efficient with our time and hers. She first takes us into a small library room with ancient books, and quickly I am actually holding a small seal possessed by Thomas Ken (1637–1711), the subject of our visit, once owned by the famous English poet and preacher John Donne (1572-1631).

We next visit the chapel, famous for its East window. Below it are stalls where the boys' choir, successors of those sixteen Choristers from the fourteenth century, continues to perform as one of the best in England. The fine wood

paneling, the stained glass, and the arched windows and ceiling represent centuries of honored tradition and quiet beauty.

Susanna then leads us to the dining center, where much of the daily life of Winchester occurs. High white walls with spaced windows rise to a dark-wood ceiling; spaces on their lower portions covered with paneling. Along the side walls are long wooden tables and benches for the younger students. On a two-step raised area at the back of the room rests a formal dining table with high-backed conservative chairs, ten on each side and two on either end. A young staff woman with red hair set in a smart short style and a full-length gray-and-black apron is setting the table with fine china, crystal glasses, and white linen napkins, which she carefully folds with her gloved hands. Covering the length of the wall behind the table is a twenty-foot-high panel with portraits of notable leaders of the school from the past.

Probably the most famous portrait in the room, however, and the one most often seen in publication, hangs on the wall just to the left of the entrance:

THOMAS KEN
(1637–1711)
SCHOLAR 1651; FELLOW 1666–84
BISHOP OF BATH AND WELLS 1684–91

Thomas, smiling, with his right arm and hand extended across his front, his fingers delicately splayed and crossed, poses in his black-and-white silk bishop's robes and black hat.

Thomas was a small man, about five feet tall, who was born to an old and established family in Somerset. His stepsister, Anne, was married to Izaak Walton, history's most famous fly fisherman and author of *The Compleat Angler*, who gave time and influence to Thomas as a boy.

Thomas was admitted to Winchester College in 1652 during the period of English history called the "interregnum" or "Commonwealth" (1649–1660), when England was ruled by the Puritan-controlled Parliament instead of a king. That made times difficult for Anglicans like him. But he proceeded successfully through the school. Susannah shows us where, as boys will, he carved his initials in the stone under a window of a cloister walkway: "TK."

Thomas then went on to New College, Oxford, in 1654, where he made lifelong friends, worshiped privately with other Anglicans, participated in music, and was ordained a priest around 1662. After serving in Essex, the Isle of Wight, and Hampshire, he returned to Winchester in 1665 as chaplain to the bishop there and became a Fellow of the college the next year. Susannah also shows us another carving on a column, this one reading

THO
KEN
1666

but it is difficult to know who carved this one. At least it seems too high up for Thomas to have reached that spot.

Thomas also became Winchester College chaplain, and in his *Manual of Prayers for the Use of the Scholars of*

AWAKE, MY SOUL!

Winchester College he included his hymns to be sung at morning, evening, and midnight, including "Awake, My Soul, and with the Sun" and "Glory to Thee, my God, This Night." These both closed with the words which we know as the "Doxology."

Thomas was an excellent preacher and a talented man, and he advanced in his calling. Charles II named him chaplain to the wife of William of Orange at the Hague, where he defended Anglican doctrine against Catholic practice. He later served in Tangier, where he preached strongly against widespread immorality. Eventually Thomas was also appointed chaplain to Charles II himself.

Thomas was a man of nerve who didn't hesitate to speak his mind, even to the king. In 1683 when Charles announced a planned visit to Winchester along with his court, including his mistress Nell Gwynne, Thomas received word that his house had been chosen for her living quarters.

He refused to admit her, and she had to stay in the deanery instead. But the next year, when the position of bishop of Bath and Wells opened, Charles proclaimed, "Who shall have Bath and Wells but the little fellow who would not give poor Nelly a lodging!" Thomas was appointed bishop, and the following year he ministered to Charles on his deathbed.

Later, Thomas and six other bishops refused a decree from King James II they felt would compromise the Anglican Church. He spent three weeks in the Tower before being acquitted. Ironically, he later maintained loyalty to James when the king was replaced in the Glorious Revolution by William and Mary. He consequently lost his bishopric and retired to Longleat, home of his college friend Lord Weymouth, in Wiltshire. He died there on March 19, 1711, and was buried at the Church of St. John in Frome, a parish of his former diocese of Bath and Wells. His friends sang "Awake, My Soul, and with the Sun."

ALONG ADDISON'S WALK

Oxford. This ancient university and Cambridge ("the other place") not far away form our mental image of a university. Colleges everywhere would love to look like this.

Walking through Oxford is like walking through a picture: ivy-covered walls framing symmetrical windows, dozens of church spires jutting up against a somber gray sky, stone cathedrals and stained glass, centuries-old odd and treasured traditions, groups of laughing school boys in jackets and striped ties, and professors and students in robes walking to class along gravel paths that crisscross manicured lawns laid with thick green turf. On a snack bar wall in the commons I see that the 1921 rowing team, not last year's basketball team, is the focus of Oxford athletic memory. There are two long oars beneath five odd-looking objects, which I finally identify as boat rudders. Printed on one is "Grand Challenge Cup, Henley, 1921." An old plaque nearby explains in these fading words:

THESE FIVE MAGDALEN RUDDERS WERE BEQUEATHED TO THE COLLEGE BY W.H. (BILL) PORRITT, COX OF THE MAGDALEN 1ST VIII IN 1919-21, AND OUBC COX IN 1921, '22, AND '23

The Magdalen crews in 1919, 1920, and 1921 were unbeatable. Such rowing achievements here are their Heismann trophies, but I think they remember theirs longer.

Oxford's alumni include many names famous in Western civilization, including hymnwriter Joseph Addison (1672–1719).

Joseph, though, is not known for his hymns. He was a famous essayist, journalist, and dramatist who fits comfortably in the ranks of major eighteenth-century English authors—Samuel Johnson, Henry Fielding, Alexander Pope, John Dryden—and he ultimately became England's secretary of state. But he reached that fame on a path that led here through Oxford's Magdalen College.

Each large English university is made up of several mainly independent colleges, rather as America is made

up of several independent states. Every college has its own name and separate campus and mostly operates separately to itself. Visitors cannot just walk into a college, because each one is protected with a guardhouse at the entrance. So when we arrive we give the name of our contact, Jane Eagan, conservator at the library. Jane had been recommended to me on the phone, the night before by Christine Ferdinand, fellow librarian. Interestingly, Christine is an American.

We are told that Jane is at the new library and are given general directions, so we start walking through ancient arches looking for a modern, perhaps glass-walled building, presumably the replacement of the old library. I don't see such a structure, so I ask someone (unlike most men, I don't mind doing that) and soon get there. It is, in fact, new, at least by Magdalen standards. It was built sometime in the 1800s, so it is practically still a teenager as libraries go at Oxford.

Like most college libraries on any given day, this one has many books and few students there to read them, but the arrangements for those who may come are stunning. The symmetrical precision of shelves, books, walls, windows, and

even ceiling décor through which Jane leads us would no doubt please the professors in the mathematics building.

Next we go to another hall and find a door that opens to a long flight of winding stairs. As we climb up and up, I wonder at people's stamina who work up here and make this trip several times a day. Finally we emerge into a large but secluded room with study tables, books, and papers. This place is for major historical research. Here we meet Robin Danvall-Smith, the college archivist, who in a quiet, friendly way and with no notes rehearses more than two hundred years of music history at Magdalen. I notice that he refers to John Stainer in a familiar way as "our organist" as if John were now in that role, even though he was here more than a century ago. Once a man is recognized as a university "Fellow," he never quite leaves; he's often spoken of in the present tense even though his tenure has passed.

While I chat with Robin, Paul stays on task and locates the wooded path known as Addison's Walk. Legend has it that Joseph was fond of strolling here, and such places are remembered at Oxford, even more than three hundred years later. C. S. Lewis is said to have become a believer in

Christ on this path.

Joseph of course used the old Magdalen library when he was a student here in the late 1600s. At Oxford he was recognized for his skill in writing poetry in Latin, and he would go on to become one of England's very best essay journalists. Unlike most of the writers of British hymns, therefore, he was not a churchman. He is best known as part of the literary team of Joseph Addison and Richard Steele, who published essays in two early eighteenth-century journals, the *Tatler* and the *Spectator*.

Born to a high church official and to privilege, Joseph first attended the university's Queen's College and then became a Fellow at Magdalen, staying there until 1699. His poetic skills won him a position with the Whig political party, and soon he became secretary for Ireland, then secretary of state, and finally a member of parliament.

The society of people of education and high social status in eighteenth-century England was formal and elegant: men wore wigs, ladies dressed in elaborate gowns, and social conduct followed strict rules. Writers promoted good sense

and moral behavior and were sharply critical of people who violated the codes. Regarding his essays, Joseph wrote, "The great and only end of these speculations is to banish vice and ignorance out of the territories of Great Britain." And he included devout religious behavior in his standards for society.

In 1712, in the space of two months, Joseph published four hymns in the *Spectator*, the last "The Spacious Firmament on High," based on Psalm 19:1–6. As Albert Bailey observes, he differs from the personal, intimate relationship with God expressed in the hymns of earlier writers like Isaac Watts, adopting a much more formal style and using distant terms for God, such as "the Great Original."

Paralleling the psalm, the hymn points to the skies as evidence of God's existence and power. The first verse speaks of the testimony of the sun during the day, and the second verse that of the moon, stars, and planets at night. The third verse asserts that even though these heavenly beings move silently (there was debate on that question during the Renaissance), their voice is heard "in reason's ear."

The music was later applied to the hymn by a composer as famous as Joseph Addison: Franz Joseph Haydn. In Vienna in 1798 he introduced his oratorio *The Creation*. Later during the nineteenth century the music of the chorus, entitled "The heavens are telling," also based on Psalm 19, was coupled with Joseph's poem to give us the hymn we sing today.

ALONG ADDISON'S WALK

SET ASIDE FOR THE MASTER

The Severn River runs through peaceful, rolling Worcestershire hills before cutting through the town of Stourport. Manmade canals provide access by passenger boats, bringing holiday travelers who tour and then move quietly on. But despite its pastoral setting, when we arrive I have trouble crossing the street in the fast and thick traffic. We also face some challenge finding Astley church, where Frances Havergal (1836–1879) was born in the rectory and where she lies in the churchyard. We actually spend awhile at the wrong church until the staff at the public library gets us back on track.

These ladies know about Frances. In a plain filing cabinet they have what may still be the best collection of material about her, including an anonymous tender-but-accurate booklet, perhaps written by one of her sisters. I know I will never find it again elsewhere, so I copy all twenty-four pages by feeding British coins into the photocopier.

Frances is a leading woman hymnist in the popularity of her hymns, though one scholar is probably right in saying her winning personality, not her literary skills, accounts for much of her fame. She is the writer of intimate lyrics featuring the first-person pronoun: "I Bring My Sins to Thee," "Is It for Me?" "Lord, Speak to Me," and "Take My Life and Let It Be," songs sung as often as any in Anglican and American churches.

Frances was exceptional in talent and consecration. The youngest child of William Henry Havergal, rector of Astley and himself a hymnwriter, she was single-mindedly fixed on Christ from early childhood. At first, as with many other sensitive children, her faith led to guilt from her feelings of not being close enough to Jesus. But through a variety of experiences she grew ever more convinced of His love and salvation. An attractive woman, she received several marriage proposals, but she turned them all down to fix herself on evangelism, music, and hymnwriting.

Born in 1836, Frances enjoyed the education and travel that her own talent and energy and the family's comfortable finances gave her. She attended boarding school at Belmont School at Campden Hill in London and at the

Powick Court school in Worcester, where children today still learn and scamper about in the cheery old building featuring differing shades of brick from various additions. Faculty cars, one a BMW, are parked close together and hug the outside walls.

The booklet says, "She probably never did a household chore in her life, and took no apparent interest in anything that was going on in the world apart from saving souls for Christ." That goal was pursued through a constant schedule of travel and a workload of Bible study, evangelism, music, and hymnwriting.

When she was sixteen, Frances moved with her family to Germany. She excelled at school, although she alienated her classmates with attempts to convert them. Much of her time was spent conducting Bible studies for people she met, whoever would listen to her. Converting souls was her passion. Ultimately she settled doubts about her own

salvation and looked forward to heaven, having no dread of death.

A return to England led to a move to Stourport and then to further travel abroad for recovery from recurring illnesses. She mastered several languages, including biblical Greek, and memorized much of the New Testament. While studying music at Cologne, Germany, she astonished her professors with her talent at the piano playing masterpieces by Beethoven and Mendelsohn.

At thirty-two Frances first traveled to Switzerland and afterwards made it a regular destination, climbing the mountains and delighting in the glorious scenery. Meanwhile she continued to write music and hymns, soon becoming famous and in constant demand. The mails filled with relentless requests from publishers and other admirers. The writing and music became intense, but for years she kept them up, along with Bible studies and evangelism. Several

SET ASIDE FOR THE MASTER

volumes of her poetry and hymns were published from 1869 to 1886.

Near the end of Frances' life, she commented to her sister Maria, "I do hope the angels will have orders to let me alone a bit when I first get to heaven!" Her last year was spent at the port city of Swansea, where she died on June 3, 1879, a few minutes after singing a hymn. She was brought home to be buried next to her father at Astley church.

It is cold and wet the day we visit there. Astley church features a squarish Norman tower at the front of a low building of irregular stones. The entrance is at its side, with a Tudor door framed by a pyramid-shaped tombstone on one side and a flowering pink shrub on the other, strangely contrasting with gargoyle faces on the cornice above. Inside is the nave where Frances ran about as a girl while her rector father was working on sermons or ecclesiastical business and where she first sang religious songs. A board announces the numbers of last Sunday's hymns. Stone arches, elaborately carved choir screens, and a worn stone font testify to the

centuries that have passed here. In one corner of the church is the elaborate tomb of a sixteenth-century local lord and his wife, their life-size figures painted in pastels lying on top, and their vertical hands holding prayer books. An inscription describes them:

HERE LIETH THE BODI OF ROBERT BLONTE
ESQUIER WHO DECEASED THE XXIII DAIE OF
MAIE AN DN 1573 AND ANNE HIS WIFE

Frances must have played around these colorful, lifeless figures often.

Outside in the wet and the fading light I look for the Havergal grave and soon find it rather close to a steep drop-off toward the road. The booklet from Stourport mentions that William Henry Havergal was buried under a fir tree, and sure enough I find a tall one crowding it on one side.

I have learned that in Britain ministers are buried under a casket-shaped sculpture with a roof-shaped top, their inscriptions prominent on one side of the roof. Henry's name

and the place and dates of his death are on the side away from the church, along with these words: A FAITHFUL MINISTER OF THE LORD.

Interestingly, on the other side of the roof, facing the church and quite prominent, are the letters FRANCES RIDLEY HAVERGAL with inscriptions of the dates and place of her death at Swansea and these words: BY HER WRITINGS IN PROSE AND VERSE SHE BEING DEAD YET SPEAKETH.

On close examination now and even a year later, while examining blown-up digital photographs of the grave, I discover that the names of William Havergal's two wives are down on the lower borders of the respective sides. Evidently when the sculpture was finally created his youngest daughter's fame merited her the prominent inscription space opposite that of her father.

Stories of Frances's compositions are many. One day when she was seventeen and a student in Germany,

she entered the study of her teacher to warm herself by the fire. There she saw a picture of Christ on the cross with the caption "I did this for thee; what hast thou done for me?" She was moved to write the words of "I Gave My Life for Thee" but was so dissatisfied with them that she threw the poem into the fire. Fortunately it bounced off a log and did not burn, and when she saved it and showed it to her father, he encouraged her to publish it.

"Take My Life and Let It Be" was written one week at Areley House in Stourport. The day we visit it we find an impressive and imposing three-story building with Greek columns on the front porch. When we go to the door we find a note with a phone number, and ringing it brings a man who identifies himself as the guard. It seems the place has been newly purchased for renovation (we see past him evidence of construction work) and he tells us, sorry, but there is no way he can let us in.

In 1874, though, Frances was in Areley House for a week, visiting there with ten friends. Not all of them were converts, however, or at least in her view not all were devout. She prayed that by the end of the week all might receive her influence, and she received her wish. Out of that week's experience she wrote one of her most famous hymns, "Take My Life and Let It Be," in which she itemizes the virtues and blessings in her life and consecrates them all to God.

One line in the hymn reads, "Take my silver and my gold; not a mite would I withhold," an allusion to the story of the poor widow in Luke 21:1–4. On one occasion she did give all of her jewelry to be used for missions. Her autobiography, *Kept for the Master's Use*, was based on this hymn.

THE SWEET SINGER OF WALES

ales beckons us: winding, shrub-lined roads lead to sweeping vistas of emerald green hills and through verdant valleys quilted into patches of centuries-old fields defined by tidy hedgerows. Driving on a Sunday afternoon through a quiet village, we pause at a tiny park where a bench back inscribed with Welsh words—"WEDI EL GYFLWYNO GAN GYNGOR BWRDEISDREF BRYCHEINIOC"—commemorates the end of World War II. Farther on, a bridge crosses a lazy river where two boys maneuver a small boat, their limited journey monitored carefully from the bank by their watchful father.

Today we travel with relative ease: the roads are paved, the SUV is air conditioned, and the modulated woman's voice from the programmed GPS tells us precisely where to turn. Two hundred years ago there were more obstacles, but they did not hinder the travels of a beloved preacher, the writer of nearly nine hundred Welsh hymns.

During the Great Awakening religious movement of the early eighteenth century, William Williams (1717–1791), influenced by the preaching of Howell Harris, became an itinerant evangelist. Over a ministry career of forty-three years he rode horseback ninety-five thousand miles throughout Wales, preaching to crowds of more than ten thousand people. Today, though, William is primarily remembered as the "Sweet Singer of Wales" who composed one of our most beloved hymns, a hymn about a journey: "Guide Me, O Thou Great Jehovah."

The hundreds of preaching tours of William Williams began from one place, his farm near Llandovery. The old gray farmhouse is still there, looking over a carefully tended valley surrounded by shaded hills and grazing sheep. As we exit our car, a van of young adults and children pulls in behind us, driven by a smiling, ruddy gentleman in a worn sport coat and plaid cap. He is Thomas William Cecil Williams, sixth-

WILLIAM WILLIAMS

generation descendant of his composer-preacher namesake.

William smiles at hearing again from us what he has heard from hundreds of visitors before, but he seems as pleased as if we were the first. (The Williams family is now into its sixth large register book for guests.) So is Cynthia, his wife of nearly forty years, who in her quaint smock and simple housedress is the quintessential grandmother. Proud of her home and family but full of questions about our own children and lives, she guides us through the ancient house, showing the clock, piano, and teapot of her husband's famous ancestor as well as wedding photos of her own three daughters. Constantly beside her is the shy, smiling, little red-haired boy who represents the eighth Williams generation.

Other members of the farm family are four black-and-white border collies, those highly intelligent and energetic dogs that are invaluable staples of Welsh sheep farms. One of them looks out unhappily from his confinement in an outbuilding. Here, William tells us, his fifth-great-grandfather stabled the faithful horse that he rode throughout Wales preaching.

William Williams knew about journeys, and his extensive travels contributed to the theme of his most famous hymn. "Guide Me, O Thou Great Jehovah" portrays Christians like us as pilgrims traveling through the difficulties of life, comparing us to the Israelites wandering through the wilderness. Just as they needed the manna, the water from the rock, and the guidance of the cloud and pillar of fire, so we, too, need God's sustenance and direction. And just as they relied on Him to lead them over Jordan into Canaan, so we trust Jehovah to carry us over death into heaven.

THE SWEET SINGER OF WALES

AT THE SOUND OF THE BELLS

William Kethe (c.1510-1594) was a fighter. We don't know when he was born or even exactly where, but he was contemporary with Shakespeare and so got mixed in with all the religious battles surrounding King Henry VIII's various ruling children. He was definitely one-sided, a Puritan rector and writer, who was dead set on fighting Catholic influence and power.

Henry VIII's one surviving son was King Edward VI, and sometime during his reign, around 1548, William wrote a poem entitled "A Ballet Declaring the Fal of the Whore of Babylone Intyuled 'Tye thy Mare, Tom Boye,' " a satire against the Catholic church. It was a clear sign of his personality and his future as a writer.

This combative attitude really heated up when Henry's Catholic daughter Mary I, known to history as "Bloody Mary" for her persecution of Protestants, came to

the throne in 1553. William promptly left the country for Germany and joined John Knox in opposing the use of the 1552 Anglican *Book of Common Prayer*, regarded as pro-Catholic. John Calvin in Switzerland approved, and soon William and his fellow Puritans left for Geneva to join Calvin's congregation there.

But during these years William had another interest besides radical opposition to the queen's religion. He was a talented poet and translator, and his renderings of the Psalms were included in the 1561 Anglican worship manual, *The Forme of Prayers and Ministration of the Sacraments Approved by J Calvyn*. It included twenty-five psalm versions, including his most famous and enduring, "All People That on Earth Do Dwell," a translation of Psalm 100, affectionately known later as "Old Hundredth." All his psalms were included in the Scottish Psalter of 1564 and some in the English Psalter of 1562. Likely he also participated in the translation of

the Geneva Bible of 1560, the most popular version in England before the King James Bible of 1611.

After Mary's death and the accession of Protestant Queen Elizabeth I in 1558, William was also free to come back to England, where by 1561 he became rector of Child Okeford Inferior church in Dorset. There he kept attacking anyone who supported the Catholics as well as Dorset sinners engaged in "abuse of the Sabbath daye, bulbeatings, beare-beatings, bowlings, dicying, cardying, daunsynges, drunkenness, whoredome," and other sins. William died in 1594 and is buried somewhere in the Child Okeford churchyard, though his grave is not marked.

According to the local historian's spiral-bound booklet on Child Okeford, the community dates back at least to the thirteenth century. Even the name has developed different spellings and disputed meanings over the centuries: try Acford, Chyld Akford, Child Acford, Chyldgaakford, Chylde Hanford, Child Ocford, Chillacford, Chyld Okeford, Child Ockford, Chele Aukford, and Child Okeford. All of these variations came because people in those centuries just spoke; they did not write. We can thank Dr. Samuel Johnson in the late eighteenth century for beginning to corral the words for consistent spelling. The word Childe (or Chyld(e) or Child) was a title for a young noble; the Acford part is a term for a set of villages.

The history says there may have been a church here since Saxon times (eleventh century or so); the ruling lord of the region presented his relative as the first rector in 1297. (There's a list of every rector since then to the right of the door: William Kethe was in office 1561–1608.) Eventually the church was named after St. Nicholas, the same one as our Santa Claus. The story of his throwing three bags of gold coins into the home of three poor girls is also in the history.

When we arrive at the building on a low hill—stone, with a looming clock tower—we wind around the front to the south side entrance. It is quiet everywhere in Child Okeford. They claim a person's voice can be heard all the way into town from a nearby hill. In the churchyard are twelve old

yew trees (yew is the wood from which English craftsmen make the English longbow), one tree for each of the twelve apostles.

Inside the church a married couple and another lady are cleaning the building. It is nice to encounter somebody: most of the time these country churches are empty when we arrive. They cheerfully point out valued treasures. One is a four-centuries-old copy of the Bishop's Bible, the official Bible in use in England before the King James Version. William Kethe would have used this very copy during the time that he was rector.

In addition to William, another famous musician associated with the church is Sir Arthur Sullivan of the celebrated operetta team Gilbert and Sullivan. He composed the tune "Gertrude" for Sabine Baring-Gould's "Onward Christian Soldiers" (see pages 90-93), and the hymn was probably first performed here at the church.

St. Nicholas offers a fine example of a special feature of English country churches—the art of bell ringing. Most of us have seen clips of this practice in movies, but to witness a performance or a practice of bell-ringers is to appreciate how complex the art is. Bells are not only rung to mark the time of day but as a part of weekly worship and, on various occasions, of local or national celebration.

Basically a set of bells—three to eight in number and of different sizes and tones—is rung in some or all of the possible mathematical variations, each called a "change." It takes hours to ring a complete "peal" using six or eight bells, though that is rarely attempted. When in England, with some investigation you can find out what night a given church's bell ringers practice and go watch them. Likely you will be the only visitor, so you can get an up-close look and listen as the men and women ringers pull on their assigned ropes. Letting go of the rope at the right moment is highly important, because a one-ton bell as it turns over could easily pull a ringer who held on too long up toward the steeple.

Ringers are organized in guilds, and it takes several years to become an accomplished ringer. On June 2, 2002, the Salisbury Diocesan Guild of Ringers rang a 1272 peal on St. Nicholas's bells in fifty minutes to celebrate Queen Elizabeth II's Golden Jubilee. William, no doubt, loved this musical tradition.

A SONG OF CELEBRATION

Philip Doddridge (1702–1751)—Congregationalist preacher, educator, writer, and composer of hymns—must have had a lighter side somewhere, but with a man that focused and hardworking, I have trouble picturing it. Here is a man who rose at five every morning to prepare for the students at his academy, and even when he was shaving, he would have one of them read to him so no time would be wasted.

The Northampton church today, standing on the spot where he preached, also appears designed for solemn, ever-productive work. Castle Hill United Reformed Church, built on the rise where the Anglo-Saxons first erected a church and the Normans later built a castle, is a two-story brown stone structure with numerous but dark arched windows and a surrounding stone wall and iron gate.

Keith Morrison, the current minister, shows us around. He is young, has a short beard and casual haircut, and wears a black fleece sweater good for cool weather. The auditorium is tastefully styled and handsomely furnished, but firmly Protestant, with strong brown pews closed on the ends to head off chilly drafts. A balcony overlooks the main floor from the sides and back. The altar area, marked off by railing, is nicely decorated but not ornate. Upstairs, organ pipes of various sizes rise on either side.

Keith takes us first into a side room to talk about Philip Doddridge. It contains a small organ, maybe for choir practice, and various other objects. In one corner, holding a large, old Bible, stands a small, simple pulpit; Keith tells us it is Philip's. There are no elaborate Anglican embellishments here, just the plain pulpit of a Non-conformist whose life began hard.

Philip was the twentieth child of Daniel and Monica Doddridge. Only he and one sister survived past childhood. He later recalled how his mother taught him Bible stories

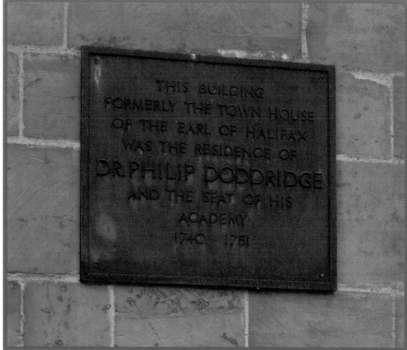

from the pictures on the blue-and-white Dutch tiles of the fireplace. But both parents were dead by the time he was thirteen, and an appointed guardian wasted what little inheritance Philip was supposed to get. Fortunately, a kind friend arranged for him to attend the Dissenting Academy at Kibworth in Leicestershire. He performed so well that, after being ordained in 1723, he became pastor of the Kibworth church.

On the death of the Kibworth Academy head master, Philip was himself appointed head of a new school. But just as he began this work, he received an invitation to serve as minister for the Castle Hill church in Northampton. In the decisive, aggressive manner he followed all his life, he not only moved there but took his academy with him, housing it for a while in his own home before moving it to Sheep Street. In time he would become one of the most recognized educators in England for his educational theories, receiving honorary degrees in his own country and contributing to the programs at Yale and Princeton in America.

Under Philip's preaching the crowds at Northampton grew. He diligently performed pastoral duties, visited members for four hours a day, and especially paid attention to young people. Through all he was a man not only of extraordinary drive and work but of strong personal devotion and prayer. In Northampton he also met Mercy Maris, whom he joined in a very happy marriage.

In addition to his preaching at church and teaching at the academy, Philip was constantly writing, not only the essays on religious controversy people expected from a Dissenter, but sermons, books, and his own paraphrased translation of the Bible. These were heavy productions, in content and in literal pounds. In a room behind the altar Keith opens for us an original copy of the fourth volume of *The Family Expositor: Or a Paraphrase and Version of the New Testament, with Critical Notes, and a Practical Improvement of Each Section.*

From what I see in the cluttered room, though, not many Doddridge mementos remain, and in this

working church they are not on organized display. There are bookcases, displays of historic communion sets, files, cardboard boxes, photographs of past members, and miscellaneous pieces of furniture. Several plaques and paintings awaiting hanging rest on the floor, including one entitled "Doddridge's Church: Honor Roll." A couple of expensively framed portraits—one of Philip—lean against bookcases. Another, the one most often seen in books and on the Web, hangs alone on one wall.

There are still memorials to Philip in the town on sites where his academies met. On one wall of the corner of a worn brick building hangs a steel plaque:

THIS BUILDING
FORMERLY THE TOWN HOUSE
OF THE EARL OF HALIFAX
WAS THE RESIDENCE OF
DR. PHILIP DODDRIDGE
AND THE SEAT OF HIS
ACADEMY
1740–1751

Business signs on the adjoining corner wall reveal that the building is currently occupied by a GENTS HAIR DRESSER next to Northamptonshire's Multi-Cultural Community Radio Station.

Perhaps the settings of these memorials are especially

appropriate. This kind of working-class urban community resembles the one Philip served. Nearby Sheep Street (now Sheaf Street), another site for his academy, was named for its industry, not for its pastoral beauty. Part of the site remains; appropriately, a church stands there now.

Philip met the famous hymnwriter Isaac Watts (see pages 38-41) around 1728, and the two became good friends. Issac had opened the way to lyrical hymns expressing the writer's personal feelings. The younger Philip followed that model to serve his simple listeners, regularly writing a hymn for them to sing at the close of each sermon. In the end he left over four hundred hymns in manuscript, and about 375 were published. Even the best of these are sung infrequently today, but one is especially familiar in American churches, a song of celebration of a Christian's day of salvation, "O Happy Day."

THE TRIUMPH SONG!

Most of our visits related to the great British hymns take us to humble places: small country churches, farm houses, quiet cemeteries.

Not today.

Lew Trenchard Manor is now a luxury hotel on the edge of the Dartmoor tors in Devonshire. As we walk from the parking area through the stone balustrades onto the lawn, the manor house appears to our left: a two-story Jacobean mansion with gray-slate façade, leaded windows, symmetrical columns and archways, a fountain in the forefront, and a lawn of manicured gardens, pools, flowers, and statuary. Entering the arched doorway and walking across the slate floor, we find a lobby with a large, ornate fireplace, polished antique furniture, intricate ceiling plasterwork, and over-stuffed sofas—details that produce a quiet, exquisite English country ambience.

Lew Trenchard is the home of the Baring-Gould

family and still belongs to them, although it is now leased to a hotel company. Dating to the early 1600s, its history includes both respectable and scandalous characters. But by far its most famous resident was Sabine Baring-Gould (1834–1924)—squire, parson, benefactor, eccentric aristocrat, hugely prolific author, and writer of two of England's most well-known hymns, "Onward Christian Soldiers" and "Now the Day Is Over."

We have no appointment today, but when we explain to the director our purpose, she graciously offers us a tour. Climbing the great curving staircase to the second floor, we come to a spacious hallway where Sabine gave parties for the parish children. The hallway opens into a luxurious bedroom once occupied by Henrietta Marie, wife of King Charles I (1600-1649). Some guests also claim to have seen here the manor's resident ghost, Margaret, an acerbic old lady of the Baring-Gould family who died in 1662 and is buried in the

parish church.

Most stories, though, center on Sabine—the "squireson," who was both squire of the estate and parson of its church. The privilege of being squire came from his birth into England's landed gentry. As the son of a wealthy and wandering father, Sabine traveled Europe, eventually finishing studies in Clare College Cambridge and returning to Lew Trenchard to supervise benevolently if overtly the people of his manor as both their squire and spiritual guide.

Details of Sabine's life show his kind but unusual and sometimes controlling personality. For one thing, he was a bit of an eccentric, sometimes teaching school with a pet bat perched on his shoulder. He also occasionally used his rank to obtain appropriations and adjustments to make building enhancements he desired. For instance, he once replaced a tenant's handsome window unit with a lesser one so that the more attractive one could be installed at his manor.

Sabine's supreme and most famous act of control, however, transpired when he came to admire a young mill girl named Grace Taylor, who was undoubtedly beautiful but not sufficiently accomplished for the role he envisioned for her. So he had her sent to school to learn to speak and pronounce English properly, and then he married her. George Bernard Shaw later used the couple as models for Professor Henry Higgins and flower girl Eliza Doolittle in his play *Pygmalion*, later made into the onstage musical and then motion picture *My Fair Lady* starring Rex Harrison and Audrey Hepburn.

The operation of Lew Trenchard and its luxurious lifestyle was expensive to maintain. Fortunately Sabine's great love of knowledge and interest in a wide spectrum of topics, coupled with his seemingly boundless energy, led to his writing a huge number of books, novels, pamphlets, and articles. Notably, he produced the multi-volume *Lives of the Saints* and assembled an important collection of folk songs.

In an outbuilding of the manor called the Folly, Sabine would stand at a high writing desk (now on display in the mansion) and churn out page after written page. Scholars estimate that he created more than two hundred book-length publications, excluding articles. Sabine Baring-Gould is credited with having, at one point, more titles catalogued in the library of the British Museum than any other writer.

Of all Sabine's compositions, however, one is by far the most widely known. He wrote it before coming to live at Lew Trenchard, hurriedly producing it in one night as an occasional piece. He had arranged for a group of children to march behind him the next day, Whit-Sunday, as he carried a cross from one church to another, and he needed a spiritual marching song to urge them along. Unable to find anything suitable, he wrote his own.

"It was written in great haste," he later said, "and I am afraid some of the rhymes are faulty. Certainly nothing has surprised me more than its popularity."

As it stands, the hymn is one of the Christian world's all-time favorites, "Onward, Christian Soldiers."

ETCHED IN STONE, ETCHED IN HEARTS

The white beaches of Brighton on England's southern coast bask under blue skies and brilliant sunlight shimmering on green sea and white Georgian buildings. It is where Britons come to play; and stately Westfield Hall, seat of town government, closely manages both recreation and propriety behind a bright red door with guarded access. After a bit of negotiation, we get permission to photograph the interior. For in the nineteenth century this house was Westfield Lodge, family home of Charlotte Elliott (1789-1871), author of "Just As I Am," evangelists' favorite hymn for stimulating audiences to respond to Christ.

As a young woman, Charlotte was healthy, happy, and witty; then a debilitating disease in 1821 left her depressed and feeling useless. But a visit the next year by preacher Cesar Moran changed her attitude, and she confessed to him that she wanted to come to Jesus but did not know how. His response, "You have only to come to Him just as you are,"

prompted one of our most beloved worship songs.

Apparently, Charlotte actually wrote "Just As I Am" some twelve years later in 1834 to support her brother Henry's project to build a school in Brighton for the daughters of clergymen. Today, St. Mary's School bravely looks out on the sea as it continues to fulfill that very mission, the main building fronted by scaffolding (the weather-beaten walls no longer support plastering) and a row of rose bushes along the façade. The red ones on the far left, we are told, were planted 175 years ago when the school began.

Inside, early-teens girls in gray uniforms scamper busily up rambling stairways as we are escorted by a cheerful and decisive head mistress, Ms. Meek. Before handing us off to Matthew, one of the teachers, for our tour, she offhandedly mentions a detail that turns out to be a highlight of our visit. Over in the athletics area, she says, is a sports equipment hut that stands on old tiling. This, local history says, was the floor of the room where Charlotte penned "Just As I Am."

We enjoy Matthew's tour, but what we really want to

see now is that little storage hut. When we get to it, there seems little to photograph, but after we finish and leave I steal a minute to run back and stand for a few seconds on that tile. Here was the place, I muse, the actual place where Charlotte wrote the hymn that thousands of worshippers have sung for nearly two hundred years.

We end our visit to St. Mary's at the old chapel building. It differs from the dignified Anglican chapels of England's churches and cathedrals. In keeping with the practical purpose of the institution, this one is used not only as a place for religious services but as a school hall and testing center. Rows of desks occupy the nave, one of them passing right under the small-but-ornate raised pulpit. Precisely centered before the altar stands a large examination clock.

Three times a year, Matthew tells us, the students assemble in the chapel for Founders Day. A member of the Elliott family always serves on the board of directors, and every Founders Day the girls hear the story of Charlotte Elliott and her hymn and sing it together. "Just As I Am" is in the original fabric of St. Mary's.

Charlotte is buried at St. Andrews church in Hove, near Brighton. There are two St. Andrews churches in town, however, and our first visit is to the wrong one. St. Andrews where Charlotte lies is nearer the beach, its churchyard a small oasis from the busy street a few feet away. A Norman tower looms over crowded ornate gravestones, including that of George Everest, for whom the world's highest mountain is named.

Charlotte's name is only one of several on the Elliott family crypt, listed under the considerably more elaborate inscriptions of her ancestors, including her father and mother. The inscription below identifies this crypt as the burial place "also of Charlotte Elliott, daughter of that same Charles and Eling Elliott." Time and weather have done their work, prying out the metal that originally filled some of the engraved letters of her given name, and on this June day of our visit green weeds partially hide the inscriptions. Still, her contribution to the music of the church follows, etched there in the stone:

AUTHOR OF "JUST AS I AM"
AND OTHER VALUED HYMNS.

ETCHED IN STONE, ETCHED IN HEARTS

SWEET MUSIC FROM THE MISTY MOORS

The whole countryside in this part of Yorkshire is—in a word—bleak. Gray is the main color, as if a child who had just one crayon drew it. As we drive into the town of Hebden Bridge, I notice a deserted factory building perched on the bank of a turbulent river. It's gray, too, with four stories of identical rectangle windows that never dreamed of a curtain. It's the kind of factory where a Dickens character like Oliver Twist would work all day before going home to a bowl of cold oats. This is not the part of England where white curly-wooled sheep graze over emerald green pastures and tourists in North Face parkas trek happily along the trails. Here it's hills, rocks, and overcast skies.

And just because it is that way, the place draws us in by its forbidding mystery. Only ten miles over the hills is Haworth, where the moors lie in thick, gray mists and where Emily Brontë wrote *Wuthering Heights*. Heathcliff was born out of this furze.

Like other hard places where life was tough years ago, Hebden Bridge gave way to a whole different culture in the late twentieth century. Today it is an arts center, where new residents have come to write and paint to capture the morose and changing scene. But in 1750 the residents were not artists. They were described as living in "a wild and inhospitable part of the country, where civilization was in low state, and where there was little of the fear or knowledge of God."

Still, a few of the farmers had a sense that they needed God, and that year they built a cheap, small, and uncomfortable chapel on donated land at Wainsgate, a community on the hills overlooking Hebden Bridge. Here, in 1763, John Fawcett (1740–1817) came to preach.

Born at Lidget Green, near Bradford, Yorkshire, John was greatly influenced as a child by Bunyan's *Pilgrim's Progress* and eventually was converted by George Whitefield. He joined the Methodists for a time, then became a Particular Baptist and was ordained a minister. When he and his wife, Susanah, arrived at Wainsgate, he served so well and kindly

JOHN FAWCETT

that the people came to love them. But the salary of twenty-five pounds per year was hardly adequate, and when an offer came in 1772 from the large Carter Lane church in London, John accepted.

What evidently happened next is not corroborated by John's writings or by direct testimony of anyone present at Wainsgate at the time, but the story passed down is this. The night before the family was to leave, anticipating the sadness of leaving his flock, John wrote a hymn that contained these words:

> When we asunder part,
> It gives us inward pain;
> But we shall still be joined in heart
> And hope to meet again.

But the next day, after having the wagon packed and climbing in with their children, John and Susanah looked at the sad, weeping church members around them and hesitated. Susanah said, "O John, I know not how to go." And he replied, "Nor I, and we shall not go. Unpack the wagon, and put everything back in its place."

John stayed at Hebden Bridge another forty-five years, preaching, teaching, and composing other hymns, including "Lord, Dismiss Us with Thy Blessing." He became so famous locally that a new building was erected on the Wainsgate hill with a large auditorium complete with balcony to accommodate the crowds.

Walking in and around Wainsgate church is sobering to me. The front is made of foreboding gray stones laid in exact symmetry, looming out at me with a sparse number of widely spaced windows that fail to give much of a welcome feeling. It all seems pretty grim.

Inside, though, there are taste and décor. An elaborate altar area with large organ pipes and an elevated marble pulpit and staircase look out over dark, rich wooden pews, some enclosed in booths. Stained-glass windows decorate the first floor, while in the balcony, covering nearly all of the side and rear walls, arched windows admit a surprising amount

of light from their stern counterparts on the outside. In the foyer, a diagram of the auditorium with permanent marker buttons records each member's attendance.

But the most foreboding and fascinating part of John Fawcett's Wainsgate is the churchyard cemetery. This is still a remote country churchyard in a poor region, and no one is here to mow and manicure the steep terraces of the hillside plot. Over the centuries tall trees have displaced tombstones, and grasses and vines festoon the graves and the large monuments erected two hundred years ago. It is the perfect setting for a ghost story or Gothic romance, and I keep expecting somebody from a Charles Dickens or Horace Walpole novel to peep out from behind a granite shaft. Moss covers almost the whole of one of the horizontal stones, reminding me of lines by Emily Dickinson:

And so, as strangers met a night,
We talked between the rooms,
Until the moss had reached our lips,
And covered up our names.

So John remained here with his people. But he was not a simple country parson. He established and operated several preacher training schools, and eventually he moved into Hebden Bridge to become the preacher for the Ebenezer Chapel, now the Hope Baptist Church. I found this plaque by the door of the gray stone building:

HERE FLOURISHED REV. JOHN FAWCETT, 1740–1817,
GIFTED SCHOLAR, DEVOTED PASTOR, AND INSPIRED PREACHER.

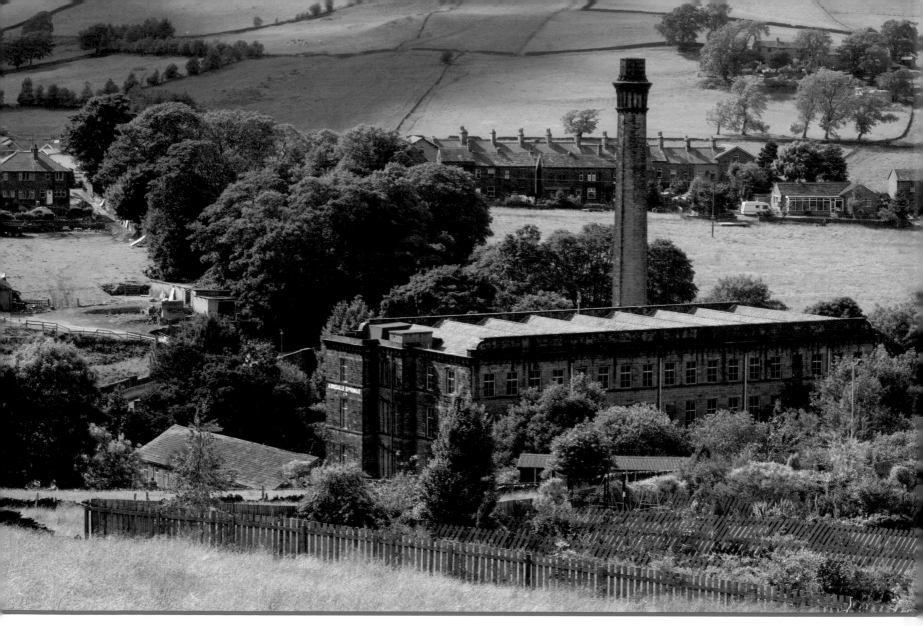

In recognition of John Fawcett, this small town minister in rural England was awarded a doctor of divinity degree in 1911 by America's Brown University.

John died on July 25, 1817, and was buried at Wainsgate. I climb above the fenced grave to read the long inscription on the dark gray stone. The years have made it hard to decipher. Susanah and two of his grandchildren are here, too. They had died before him and were first buried in Hebden Bridge, but John left orders that on his death they be disinterred and buried with him out here.

And so, as I stand looking at the stone, I think, Here they lie, close by the door of a building foreboding on the outside, but stately and beautiful within. And here in this still remote and humble place John composed perhaps the warmest and most beloved hymn on fellowship for Christians: "Blest be the tie that binds our hearts in Christian love." Amen.

SWEET MUSIC FROM THE MISTY MOORS

THE STRAINS OF TRAGEDY

We've spent a day at Southampton visiting the sites associated with Isaac Watts (see p. 38), but the morning before we leave we stop for a few minutes by the harbor. Several small sailboats rest in a row. The water is calm, the sky grayish. Mostly things are quiet today.

It was not quiet on April 10, 1912, though, when the largest passenger ship in the world sailed out of Southampton on its maiden voyage to cheering crowds and waving passengers. Among the happy sounds was the music of Wallace Hartley's band, employed on the ship for entertaining the wealthy and sophisticated first-class passengers on the voyage to New York. Five days later, as depicted in the 1997 film *Titanic*, starring Leonardo DiCaprio and Kate Winslet, Wallace leads his string quartet in playing on deck for the comfort of the terrified passengers as the ship begins to sink. As the chaos intensified, he dismisses his three colleagues so they can seek some kind of escape, but as they start to leave, he himself takes his violin and begins to play Sarah Adams' hymn, "Nearer, My God, to Thee." Hearing its soothing strains, the other musicians return one by one, and together they play until the waters on the deck rise to their feet. Wallace's last words are, "Gentlemen, it has been a privilege playing with you tonight."

Some surviving passengers said that such a scene actually occurred that cold night in 1912. But, as is often true with historical events, there is controversy over the details, including those surrounding the playing of "Nearer, My God, to Thee." Some argue that Sarah's hymn wasn't played that night at all. If it were, others say, Wallace would not have played it with American Lowell Mason's tune "Bethany," as used in the 1997 movie, but with one of two British tunes: John B. Dykes' "Horbury" or Walter Sullivan's "Propior Deo."

Regardless, Sarah's hymn is permanently connected with the tragedy, and it and Henry Lyte's "Abide with Me" are the British hymns most often sung for comfort at moments of near or present death. The deaths of at least three American presidents, two assassinated, are associated with "Nearer, My God, to Thee." William McKinley is

reported to have quoted its words as he died, and it was sung at the funerals of James Garfield and Gerald Ford. During the last century multiple *Titanic* films and celebrities have helped make it famous, and it has been translated into several languages.

Sarah was born at Harlow, Essex, on February 22, 1805, the daughter of liberal newspaper editor Benjamin Flower. She became a celebrated Romantic poet, writing the long poem "Vivia Perpetua" about the struggles of early Christians, as well as numerous other poems and several hymns. Beautiful and talented, she was also an actress, playing the role of Lady Macbeth. A Unitarian, feminist, and social activist, she wrote political and social advocacy pieces. During her life she knew several famous authors, including William Wordsworth, Percy Bysshe Shelley, Robert Browning, and Charles Dickens.

Vivacious and very independent, Sarah married William Bridges Adams in 1834 and lived with him in London. (They agreed that she would not do housework.)

There she attended Unitarian South Place Chapel at Finsbury Circus, where today elite curved apartment buildings look over a secluded public park and London bankers on their lunch break play lawn bowls on the immaculately manicured turf. William Johnson Fox was the minister there at the time, and thirteen of her hymns, including "Nearer, My God, to Thee," were published in his *Hymns and Anthems* (1841). Her sister Eliza provided the music for some of these.

Eliza became ill in 1846, and Sarah nursed her. But in the process she developed tuberculosis herself. She died in London two years later, leaving as her legacy a hymn which draws us all nearer to God.

EPILOGUE

Our journey through the great British hymns has taken us to widely different places: from the hectic streets of London to the somber quiet of a rural Wainsgate cemetery; from the serene hills of the Cotswolds to the lush mountains of Wales; from sunny Southampton to wind-beaten Whitby off the North Sea. And in these places we have met very different people: from sophisticated essayist Joseph Addison to simple lay preacher Edward Mote; from wealthy Sabine Baring-Gould to humbly endowed John Fawcett; from Anglican theologian John Keble to scholarly Dissenter Philip Doddridge; from stirring Charles Wesley to quiet Charlotte Elliott; from strong and rough seaman John Newton to refined Frances Ridley Havergal. They lived different lives in different centuries, and they experienced different fortunes in their long or short times on earth. But they all shared a belief in Christ, and they all were blessed with a gift: the power to express His grace and love in words so well crafted and so harmoniously joined that they pierce our hearts, stir our souls, and linger long in our memories.

BIBLIOGRAPHY

SOURCES

The authors gratefully acknowledge that the texts of hymns printed in this book are from the Cyber Hymnal. The biographical and historical information about the hymns and hymnwriters discussed in *Abide with Me* is taken from the following books and from articles referred to below. The authors gratefully acknowledge these sources and express appreciation to their authors. Listed also are books which may be valuable for readers interested in further study of the great British hymns. Several of these are rare volumes in the Bailey Collection in the Special Collections division of Beaman Library, Lipscomb University, Nashville, Tennessee.

BOOKS

Bailey, Albert Edward. *The Gospel in Hymns: Backgrounds and Interpretations.* Charles Scribner's Sons, 1950.

Companion to the United Methodist Hymnal. Ed. Carlton Young. Nashville: Abingdon Press, 1993.

Deacon, Malcom. *The Church on Castle Hill: The History of Castle Hill United Reformed Church, Northampton.* Northampton, England: Park Lane Publishing, 1995.

Dictionary of Hymnology: Origin and History of Christian Hymns and Hymnwriters of all Ages and Nations. 2 vols. Ed. John Julian. Rpt. of 1907 revised edition with new supplement. Grand Rapids: Kregel Publications, 1985 .

Dictionary of National Biography. London: Oxford University Press, 1937.

Dunford, C. M. *Broadhembury: A Picture of Our Parish.* 2nd edition. Cullompton, England: Arocet Press, 2000.

Giles, C. G. *St. Nicholas' Church, Child Okeford, Dorset: A Short History.* 1998.

Gospel Standard Baptist Trust, Ltd. *Diary and Selection of Hymns of Augustus Top-lady.* Ptd. By R.T. Mould & Co., Ltd., 9 Little Holme St., Leicester, England, LE3 5NG., 1969. Obtainable from Mr. O.G. Pearce; 15a Park Ave. South, Harpenden, Hertshire, England.

Johnson, Guy. *Treasury of Great Hymns and Their Stories.* Greenville, S.C.: Bob Jones University Press, 1986.

McCann, Forrest M. *Hymns and History: An Annotated Survey of Sources.* Abilene: Abilene Christian University Press, 1997.

Manning, Bernard L. *The Hymns of Wesley and Watts: Five Informal Papers.* London: The Epworth Press, 1942.

Nutter, Charles S. *Historic Hymnists: A Portrait Gallery of Great Hymn Writers.* Boston, 1893.

Peale, Norman Vincent. *My Favorite Hymns and the Stories Behind Them.* San Francisco: HarperSanFrancisco, 1994.

Reynolds, William J. *Songs of Glory: Stories of 300 Great Hymns and Gospel Songs.* Grand Rapids: Zondervan Books, Zondervan Publishing House, 1990.

Routley, Erik. *Hymns and the Human Life.* Grand Rapids: William B. Eerdmans Publishing Co., 1959.

The Musical Wesleys. Westport, Conn.: Greenwood Press, Publishers: 1968, rpt. 1976.

Rutler, George William. *Brightest and Best: Stories of Hymns.* San Francisco: Ignatius Press, 1998.

Smith, H. Augustine. *Lyric Religion: The Romance of Immortal Hymns.* New York: Fleming H. Revell Co., 1931.

Turner, Steve. *Amazing Grace: The Story of America's Most Beloved Song.* New York: HarperCollins Publishers, 2002.

Watson, J.R., ed. *An Annotated Anthology of Hymns.* Oxford: University Press, 2002.

Wright, Thomas. *The Lives of the British Hymn Writers: Being Personal Memoirs Derived Largely from Unpublished Materials. Vol. 3. Isaac Watts and Contemporary Hymn Writers.* London: C.J. Farncombe & Sons, Ltd., 1914.

ARTICLES

Online articles on the hymnwriters or on individual hymns may be accessed respectively by name or title. The authors especially acknowledge use of articles in the online edition of the *Oxford Dictionary of National Biography* and in Wikipedia.

PHOTO CAPTIONS

Cover image: Mountains above Ambleside, Lake Distict

Copyright page image: College courtyard, Cambridge, England

Audio Acknowledgements page: Church ruin, Stourport, England

Page 3   All Saints Church Hursley, Hampshire. John Keble ("Sun of my Soul") was priest of this small parish from 1836 until his death thirty years later. He is buried with his wife in the churchyard.

Page 9   St. Andrews Church, Holborn Circus, London

Page 10   Church of St. Peter & St. Paul, Olney, where John Newton was curate 1764-1780. Newton's pulpit and portrait at the back of Olney Parish Church.

Page 11   Olney vicarage and the picturesque Olney High Street

Page 12   William Cowper's writing hut at the edge of the orchard between his and Newton's homes. The upstairs window overlooking the orchard where Newton is believed to have written "Amazing Grace."

Page 13   The ornate pulpit in St. Mary, Woolnoth Church, London, where John Newton preached from 1780 and where he was originally buried with his wife, Mary.

Page 14   Olney Church

Page 15   Olney churchyard and final resting place of John Newton

Page 16   St Andrews Church and the historic village of Broadhembury, Devon

Page 17   "Rock of Ages" site near Cheddar Gorge, Somerset

Page 18   Interior of St. Andrews Church, Broadhembury. Sign in Cheddar Gorge advertising "Rock of Ages" open air service.

Page 19   St. Andrews churchyard

Page 20   View across Torbay towards Brixham from the garden of Henry Lyte's house on Berry Head. Sunset viewed from bench in Lyte's garden. Cat outside Brixham Church and exterior of Berry Head Hotel.

Page 21   Brixham harbour

Page 22   Colorful fishermen's cottages surrounding Brixham Church. Interior of Berry Head House. Brixham Church exterior.

Page 23   Berry Head Hotel, once the home of Henry Lyte

Page 24   The secluded entrance of Llanlleonfel church, Wales. John Wesley's study rooms in Oxford, his pulpit in the New Room in Bristol, and a statue of Wesley outside his church in London.

Page 25   Interior of Wesley's church in London, including the original meeting place.

Page 26   Kitchen in the Charles Wesley home in Bristol, tombstone of Charles' wife and children, and interior of Christ Church, where he was ordained.

Page 27   Charles Wesley's study, Bristol

Page 28   Interior of the New Room, Bristol

Page 29   Music Room, Charles Wesley House, Bristol

Page 30   Mountain view near Brathay, Lake District. Cross outside Holy Trinity Church, Brathay. Old Mill building Ambleside, Farm, Cumbria.

Page 31   Ambleside, Lake District

Page 32   View near Ambleside

Page 33   Lake Windermere

Page 34   Whitby Abbey and Whitby town

Page 35   Steps up to Whitby Abbey, river running through the town of Whitby

Page 36   Whitby Abbey detail

Page 37   View over Whitby, Yorkshire, towards the Abbey on the hill

Page 38   Watts Mount in Abney Park, Stoke Newington, where he sat writing many of his famous hymns. Westminster Abbey, where the earliest memorial to Watts can be found. Grave of Watts.

Page 39   The remaining tower from the church of All Hallows Staining where Watts last preached publicly before moving to Abney Park in Stoke Newington. View over Southampton water.

Page 40   Watts windows in Church of the Ascension, Bitterne Park, Southampton, commemorating seven of his most popular hymns.

Page 41   Statue of Watts on Watts Walk, Abney Park, Stoke Newington

Page 42   Punting on the River Cam in Cambridge, road cutting through hills England. Cyclist outside Stoneyard Baptist Church, Cambridge.

PHOTO CAPTIONS